Contents

Alabama

NICKNAME: Heart of Dixie

Originally part of Mississippi Territory; Georgia's claims ceded to the United States, 1802; southwestern corner annexed from Spain, 1813; Indian claims relinquished, 1814–16; Alabama organized as territory, 1817.

BOUNDARIES

North by Tennessee, east by Georgia, south by Florida and the Gulf of Mexico, west by Mississippi.

LARGEST CITIES

Birmingham (1), Mobile (2), Montgomery (3), Huntsville (4).

POPULATION: 3,444,165
RANK: 21st

TIME ZONE: Central

SONG: "Alabama"

BIRD

Yellowhammer

FLOWER

Camellia

ORIGIN OF NAME

Indian, meaning "I Clear the Thicket"

DISCOVERED

1540 by De Soto (Spanish)

SETTLED

1702 by the French near Mobile

AREA & LOCATION

51,609 square miles
29th in size

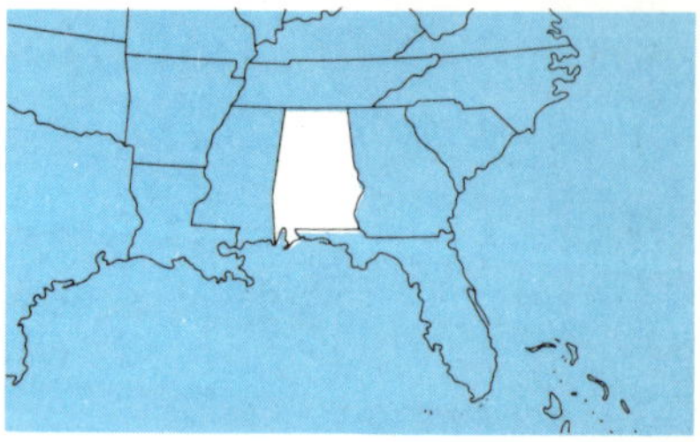

ELEVATION

High: 2,407 feet
Low: sea level

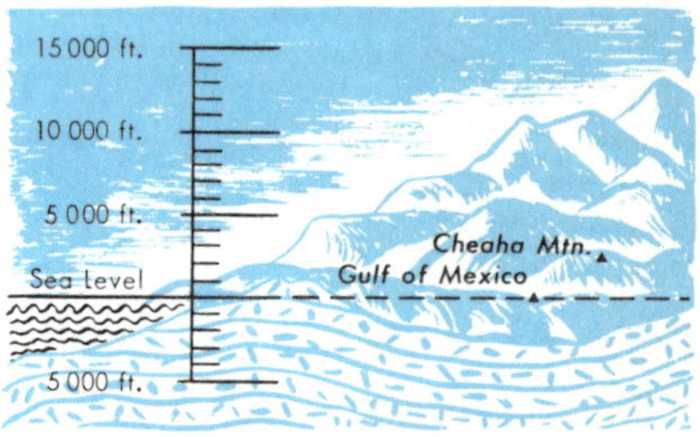

CAPITAL

Montgomery

ADMITTED TO UNION

1819 as 22nd state

SEAL & MOTTO

"Audemus Jura Nostra Defendere" ("We Dare Defend Our Rights")

Know Your USA

Compiled by GEORGE E. ROSS

RAND McNALLY & COMPANY

CHICAGO • NEW YORK • SAN FRANCISCO

ACKNOWLEDGMENTS

This publication is adapted from KNOW YOUR U.S.A., by George E. Ross—copyright, 1952, by George E. Ross.

Many of the line drawings of the capitol buildings and the state seals which appear on the State pages are reproduced from *The Book of the States*, published by the Council of State Governments, Chicago, Illinois.

Cover photographs: left, David Muench; center, David Muench; right, Rhodes Patterson

Library of Congress Catalog Card Number: 65-22220
ISBN 0-528-87738-0
Printed in the United States of America by Rand McNally & Company
Third paperback printing, 1977

Alaska

NICKNAME: Last Frontier

Purchased from Russia by the United States in 1867.

BOUNDARIES

North by the Arctic Ocean, east by Yukon, southeast by British Columbia, south by the Pacific Ocean, west by Bering Sea and Strait.

LARGEST CITIES

Anchorage (1), Spenard (2), Fairbanks (3), Juneau (4), Ketchikan (5).

POPULATION: 302,173

RANK: 50th

TIME ZONES

Southeastern part, Pacific
Yakutat vicinity, Yukon
Central part, Alaska-Hawaii
Western part, Bering
Aleutian Islands, Bering

SONG: "Alaska's Flag"

BIRD

Willow Ptarmigan

FLOWER

Forget-me-not

ORIGIN OF NAME

Eskimo, meaning "Great Land"

DISCOVERED

1741 by the Russians

SETTLED

1784 by Russians on Kodiak Island

AREA & LOCATION

586,400 square miles
1st in size

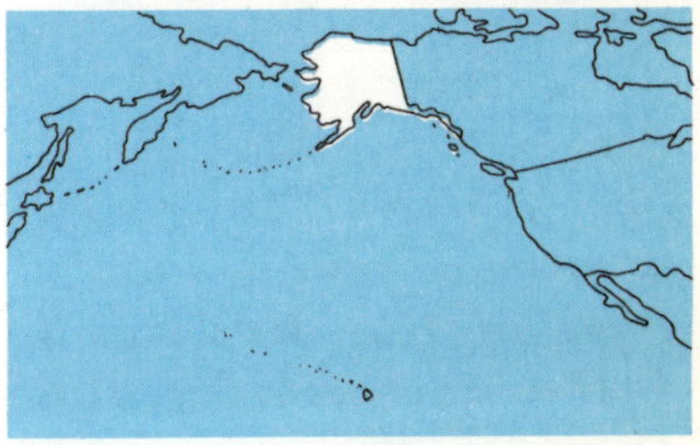

ELEVATION

High: 20,320 feet
Low: sea level

CAPITAL

Juneau

ADMITTED TO UNION

1959 as 49th state

SEAL & MOTTO

"North to the Future"

Arizona

NICKNAME: Grand Canyon State

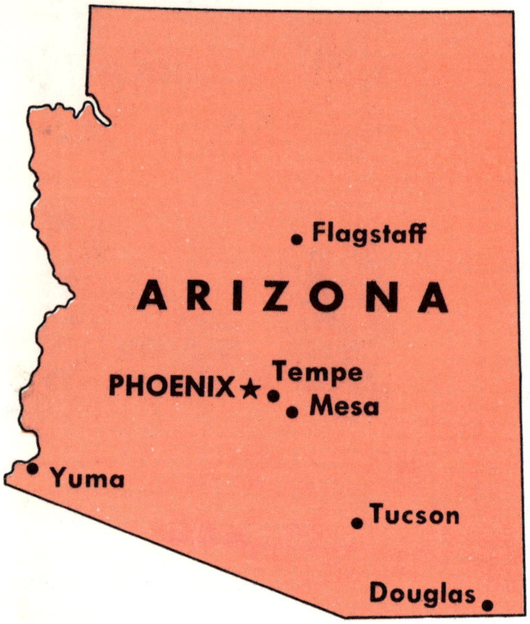

Part of the Mexican Cession of 1848; southern section part of Gadsden Purchase of 1853.

BOUNDARIES

North by Utah, east by New Mexico, south by Mexico, west by California and Nevada.

LARGEST CITIES

Phoenix (1), Tucson (2), Scottsdale (3), Tempe (4), Mesa (5).

POPULATION: 1,772,482
RANK: 33rd

TIME ZONE: Mountain

SONG: "Arizona"

BIRD

Cactus Wren

FLOWER

Saguaro Cactus

ORIGIN OF NAME

Indian, meaning "Small Spring"

DISCOVERED

1539 by de Niza (Spanish)

SETTLED

1776 by the Spanish at Tucson

AREA & LOCATION

113,909 square miles
6th in size

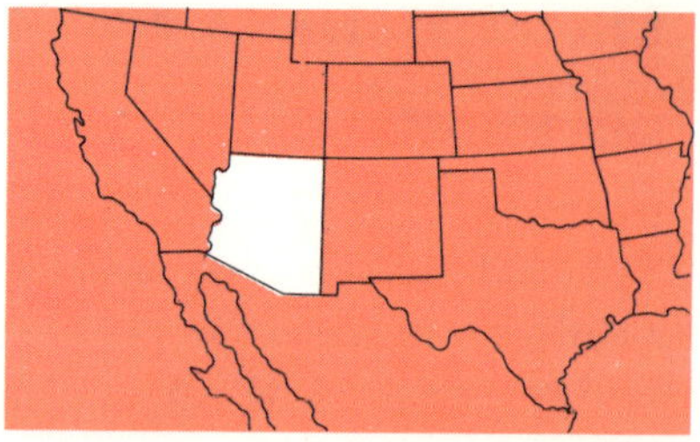

ELEVATION

High: 12,670 feet
Low: 100 feet

CAPITAL

Phoenix

ADMITTED TO UNION

1912 as 48th state

SEAL & MOTTO

"Ditat Deus" ("God Enriches")

Arkansas

NICKNAME: Land of Opportunity

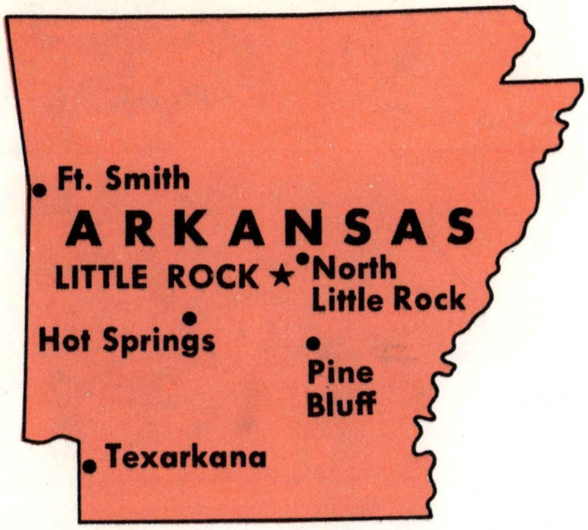

Part of the Louisiana Purchase of 1803; part of Louisiana Territory, 1804, of Missouri Territory, 1812; separate territory, 1819.

BOUNDARIES
North by Missouri, east by Tennessee and Mississippi, south by Louisiana, west by Texas and Oklahoma.

LARGEST CITIES
Little Rock (1), Fort Smith (2), North Little Rock (3), Pine Bluff (4), Hot Springs (5), Fayetteville (6).

POPULATION: 1,923,295
RANK: 32nd

TIME ZONE: Central

SONG: "Arkansas"

BIRD

Mockingbird

FLOWER

Apple Blossom

ORIGIN OF NAME
Indian, meaning is unknown

DISCOVERED
1541 by De Soto (Spanish)

SETTLED
1686 by the French at Arkansas Post

AREA & LOCATION
53,104 square miles
27th in size

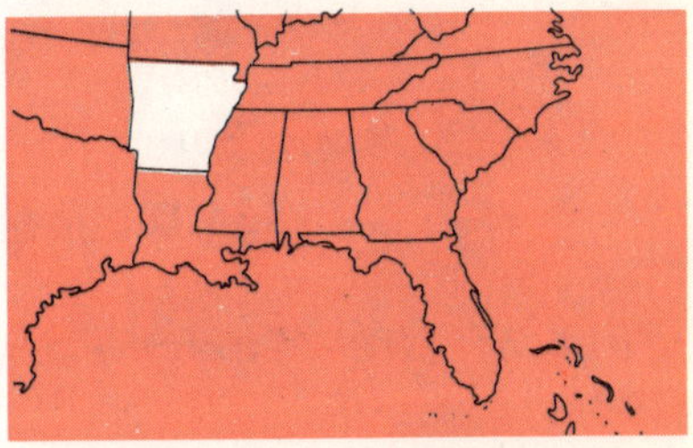

ELEVATION
High: 2,823 feet
Low: 55 feet

CAPITAL
Little Rock

ADMITTED TO UNION
1836 as 25th state

SEAL & MOTTO
"Regnat Populus"
("The People Rule")

California

NICKNAME: Golden State

Part of the Mexican Cession of 1848.

BOUNDARIES

North by Oregon, east by Nevada and Arizona, south by Mexico, west by the Pacific Ocean.

LARGEST CITIES

Los Angeles (1), San Diego (2), San Francisco (3), San Jose (4), Oakland (5), Long Beach (6).

POPULATION: 19,953,134
RANK: 1st

TIME ZONE: Pacific

SONG: "I Love You, California"

BIRD

California Valley Quail

FLOWER

Golden Poppy

ORIGIN OF NAME

Spanish, from "island near Paradise" in 16th-century novel

DISCOVERED

1542 by Cabrillo (Spanish)

SETTLED

1769 at San Diego by Spanish

AREA & LOCATION

158,693 square miles
3rd in size

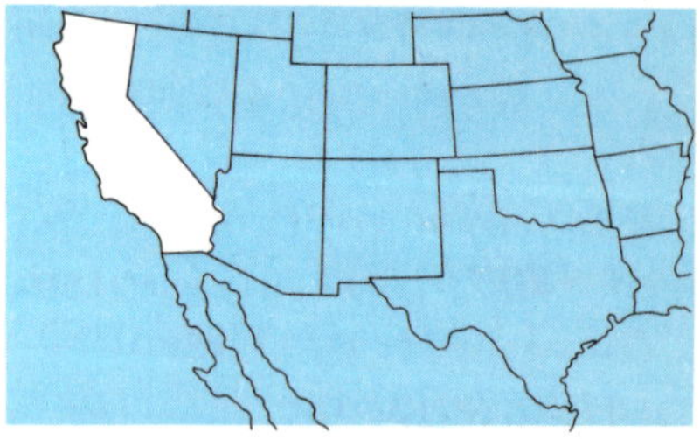

ELEVATION

High: 14,495 feet
Low: 282 feet below sea level

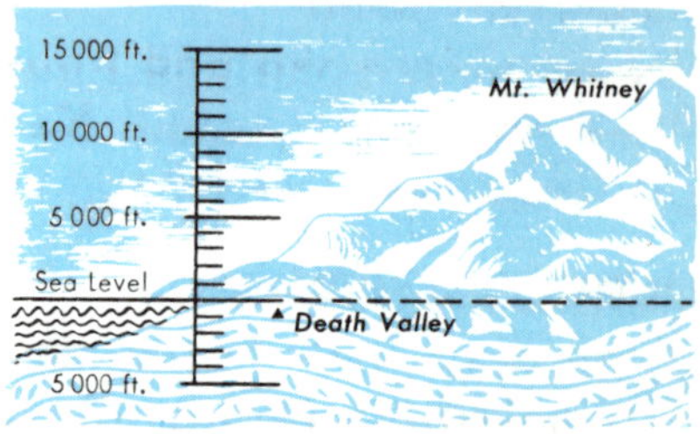

CAPITAL

Sacramento

ADMITTED TO UNION

1850 as 31st state

SEAL & MOTTO

"Eureka!" ("I Have Found It!")

Colorado

NICKNAME: Centennial State

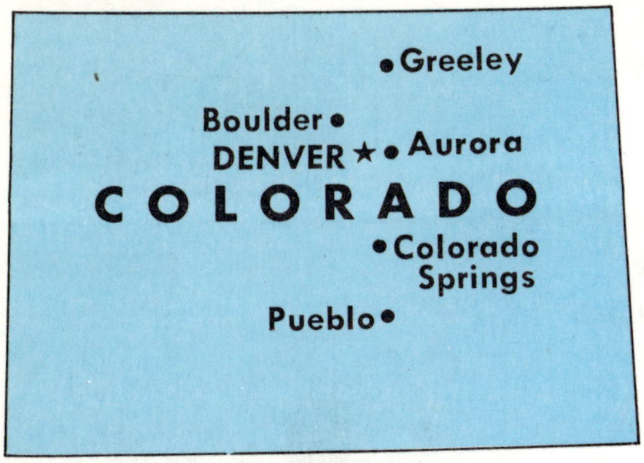

Eastern section was part of the Louisana Purchase of 1803, and the western section was part of the Mexican Cession of 1848. Area was part of Utah, Kansas, Nebraska, and New Mexico before becoming separate territory in 1861.

BOUNDARIES
North by Wyoming and Nebraska, east by Nebraska and Kansas, south by Oklahoma and New Mexico, west by Utah.

LARGEST CITIES
Denver (1), Colorado Springs (2), Lakewood (3), Pueblo (4), Aurora (5).

POPULATION: 2,207,259
RANK: 30th

TIME ZONE: Mountain

SONG: "Where the Columbines Grow"

BIRD

Lark Bunting

FLOWER

Rocky Mountain Columbine

ORIGIN OF NAME

Spanish, meaning "Red"

DISCOVERED

1541 by Coronado (Spanish)

SETTLED

1851 at San Luis

AREA & LOCATION

104,247 square miles
8th in size

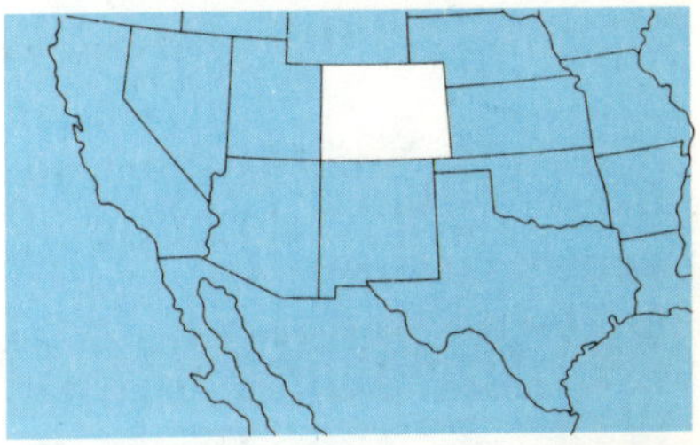

ELEVATION

High: 14,423 feet
Low: 3,350 feet

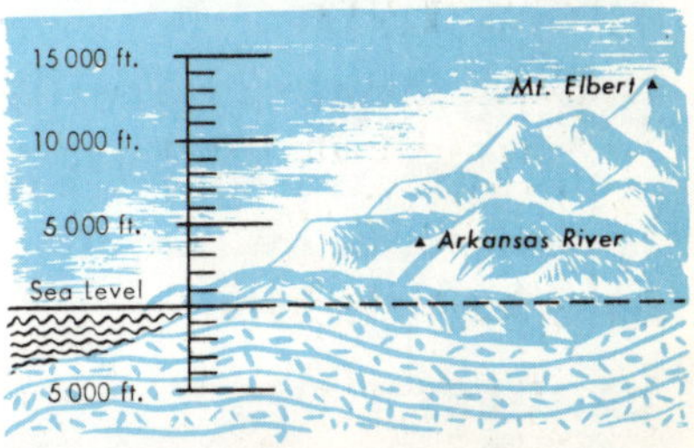

CAPITAL

Denver

ADMITTED TO UNION

1876 as 38th state

SEAL & MOTTO

"Nil Sine Numine"
("Nothing without Providence")

Connecticut

NICKNAME: Constitution State

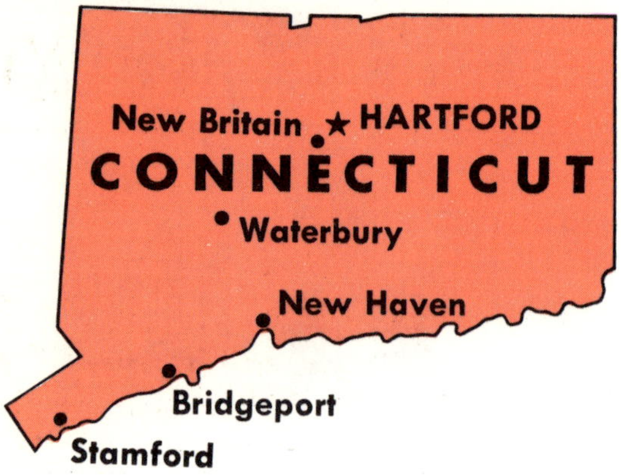

First colony to have a written constitution, the "Fundamental Orders," adopted by the Connecticut Valley towns in 1639. One of the thirteen original states.

BOUNDARIES

North by Massachusetts, east by Rhode Island, south by Long Island Sound, west by New York.

LARGEST CITIES

Bridgeport (1), Hartford (2), New Haven (3), Stamford (4), Waterbury (5), New Britain (6), Norwalk (7).

POPULATION: 3,032,217
RANK: 24th

TIME ZONE: Eastern

BIRD

Robin

FLOWER

Mountain Laurel

ORIGIN OF NAME

Indian, meaning "Long River"

DISCOVERED

1614 by the Dutch

SETTLED

1633 by English at Windsor

AREA & LOCATION

5,009 square miles
48th in size

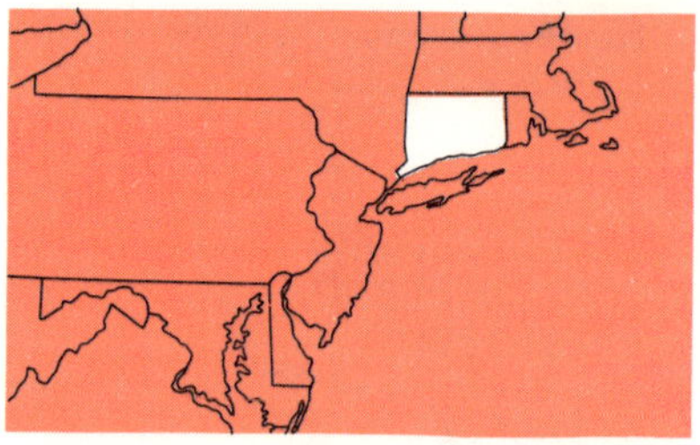

ELEVATION

High: 2,380 feet
Low: sea level

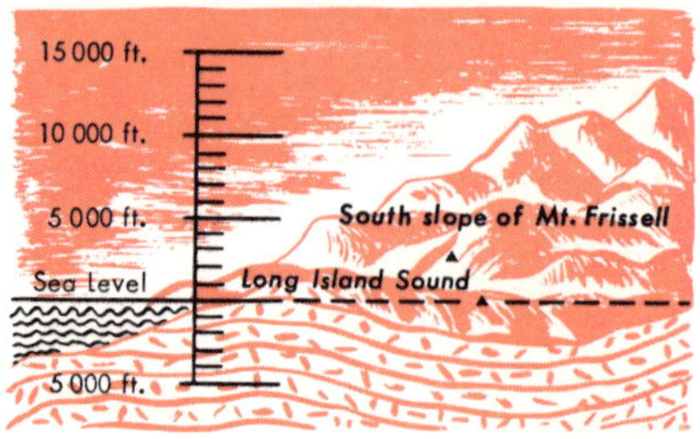

CAPITAL

Hartford

ADMITTED TO UNION

1788 as 5th of the 13 original states

SEAL & MOTTO

"Qui Transtulit Sustinet"
("He Who Transplanted Still Sustains")

Delaware

NICKNAME: First State

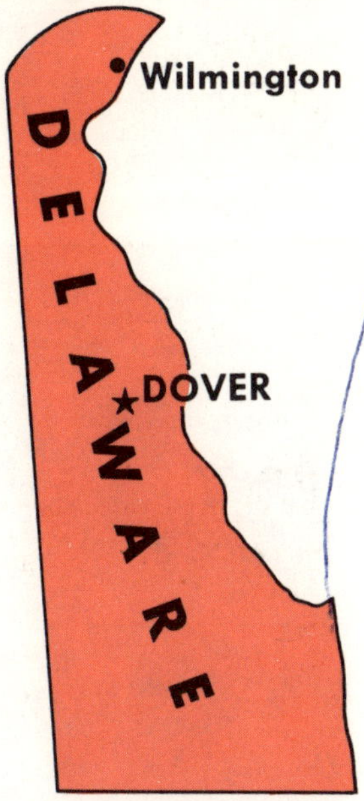

Area included in land grant of Duke of York until 1682, when it was transferred to William Penn. Colony became sovereign state in 1776. It was the first to ratify the Constitution.

BOUNDARIES

North by Pennsylvania; east by New Jersey, Delaware Bay, Atlantic Ocean; south and west by Maryland.

LARGEST CITY: Wilmington

POPULATION: 548,104
RANK: 46th

TIME ZONE: Eastern

SONG: "Our Delaware"

BIRD

Blue Hen Chicken

FLOWER

Peach Blossom

ORIGIN OF NAME

English, after Lord de la Warr

DISCOVERED

1609 by Henry Hudson (Dutch)

SETTLED

1638 by Swedes at Wilmington

AREA & LOCATION

2,057 square miles
49th in size

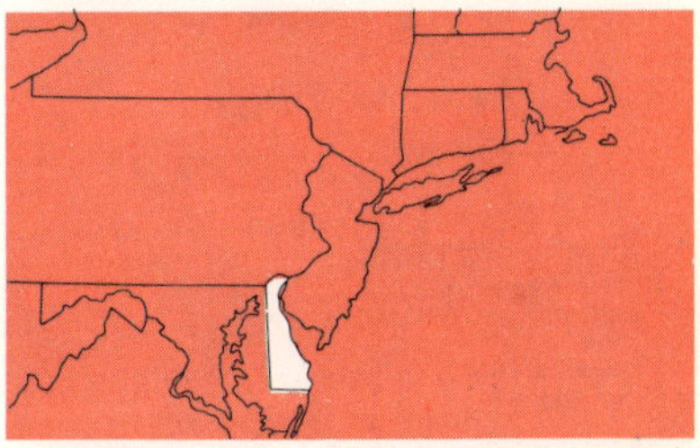

ELEVATION

High: 442 feet
Low: sea level

CAPITAL

Dover

ADMITTED TO UNION

1787 as first of the 13 original states

SEAL & MOTTO

"Liberty and Independence"

Florida

NICKNAME: Sunshine State

Florida was ceded, 1783, by England to Spain, in 1819 by Spain to the United States; became territory in 1822.

BOUNDARIES

North by Alabama and Georgia, east by Atlantic Ocean, south by the Straits of Florida, west by the Gulf of Mexico and Alabama.

LARGEST CITIES

Jacksonville (1), Miami (2), Tampa (3), St. Petersburg (4), Fort Lauderdale (5).

POPULATION: 6,789,443
RANK: 9th

TIME ZONE

Peninsula: Eastern
West Panhandle: Central

SONG: "Swanee River"

BIRD

Mockingbird

FLOWER

Orange Blossom

ORIGIN OF NAME

Spanish, meaning "Land of Flowers"

DISCOVERED

1513 by Ponce de Leon (Spanish)

SETTLED

1565 by Spanish at St. Augustine

AREA & LOCATION

58,560 square miles
22nd in size

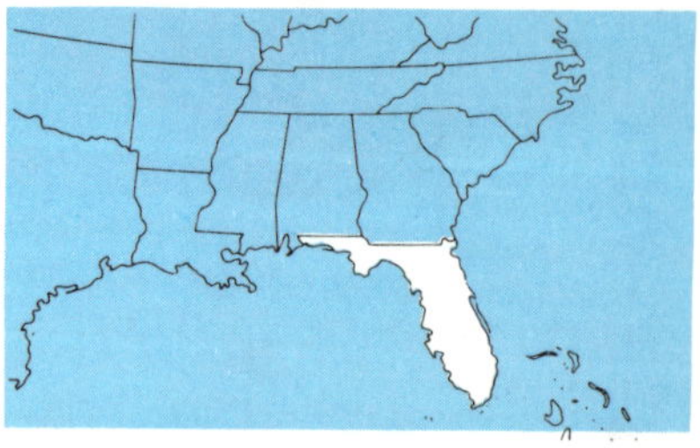

ELEVATION

High: 345 feet
Low: sea level

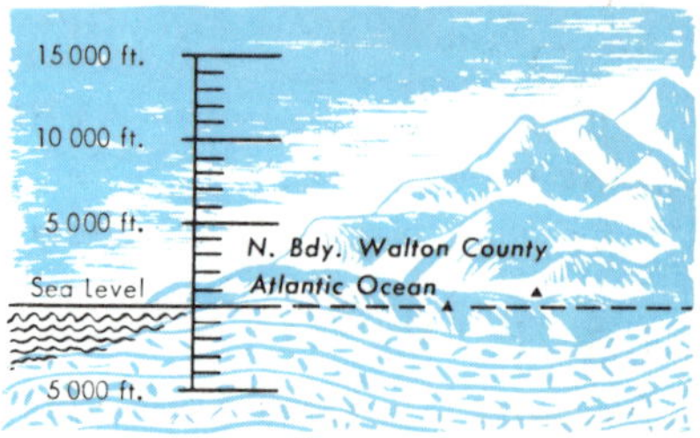

CAPITAL

Tallahassee

ADMITTED TO UNION

1845 as 27th state

SEAL & MOTTO

"In God We Trust"

Georgia

NICKNAME: Empire State of the South

One of the thirteen original states.

BOUNDARIES

North by Tennessee and North Carolina, northeast by South Carolina, east by the Atlantic Ocean, south by Florida, west by Alabama.

LARGEST CITIES

Atlanta (1), Columbus (2), Macon (3), Savannah (4), Albany (5).

POPULATION: 4,589,575

RANK: 15th

TIME ZONE: Eastern

SONG: "Georgia"

BIRD

Brown Thrasher

FLOWER

Cherokee Rose

ORIGIN OF NAME

English, in honor of King George II

DISCOVERED

1540 by De Soto (Spanish)

SETTLED

1733 by Oglethorpe at Savannah

AREA & LOCATION

58,876 square miles

21st in size

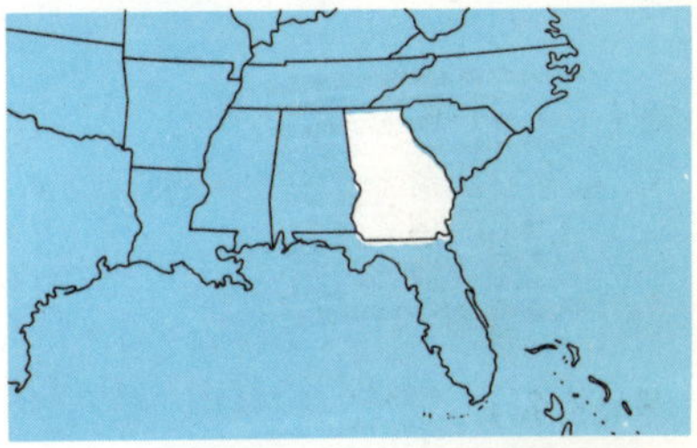

ELEVATION

High: 4,784 feet

Low: sea level

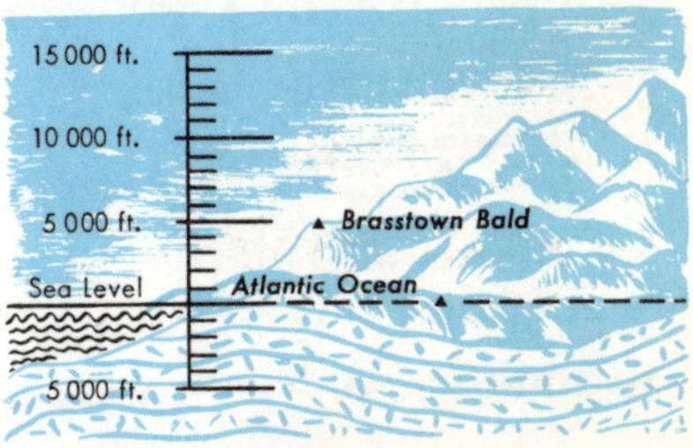

CAPITAL

Atlanta

ADMITTED TO UNION

1788 as 4th of the 13 original states

SEAL & MOTTO

"Wisdom, Justice, Moderation"

Hawaii

NICKNAME: The Aloha State

At the time Hawaii was discovered by Captain Cook, the islands were under the rule of four native kings. They were united under Kamehameha I, who was crowned as King of Hawaii in 1790. The islands were annexed by the United States in 1898.

LARGEST CITIES

Honolulu (1), Kailua (2), Kaneohe (3).

POPULATION: 769,913

RANK: 40th

TIME ZONE: Alaska-Hawaii

SONG: "Hawaii Ponoi"

BIRD

Nene (Hawaiian Goose)

FLOWER

Red Hibiscus

ORIGIN OF NAME

Polynesian, meaning uncertain

DISCOVERED

1778 by Cook (English)

AREA & LOCATION

6,424 square miles

47th in size

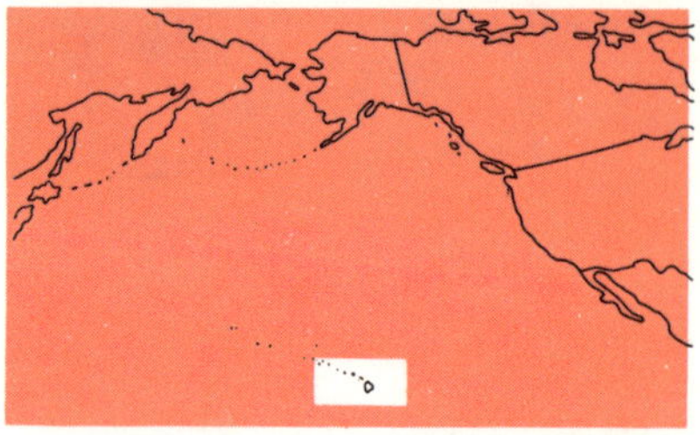

ELEVATION

High: 13,796 feet

Low: sea level

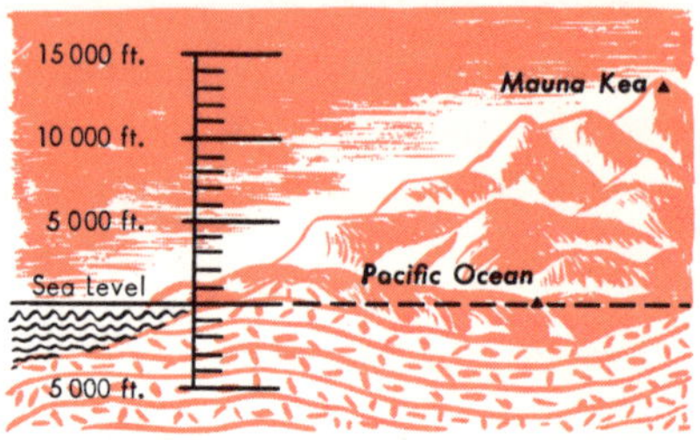

CAPITAL

Honolulu

ADMITTED TO UNION

1959 as 50th state

SEAL & MOTTO

"Ua Mau Ke Ea O Ka Aina I Ka Pono" ("The Life of the Land Is Perpetuated in Righteousness")

Idaho

NICKNAME: The Gem State

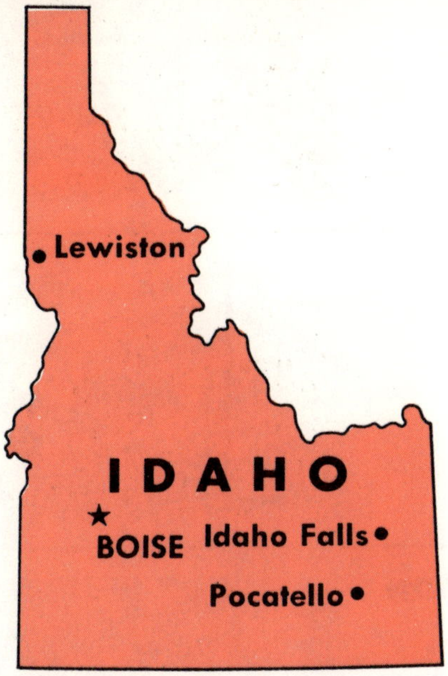

Came under American jurisdiction in 1846; organized as separate territory in 1863.

BOUNDARIES

North by British Columbia, east by Montana and Wyoming, south by Utah and Nevada, west by Oregon and Washington.

LARGEST CITIES

Boise (1), Pocatello (2), Idaho Falls (3).

POPULATION: 713,008
RANK: 42nd

TIME ZONE

North of Salmon River: Pacific
Remainder of state: Mountain

SONG: "Here We Have Idaho"

BIRD

Mountain Bluebird

FLOWER

Syringa

ORIGIN OF NAME

Indian, meaning "Light on the Mountains"

DISCOVERED

1805 by Lewis & Clark

SETTLED

1860 at Franklin by Mormons

AREA & LOCATION

83,557 square miles
13th in size

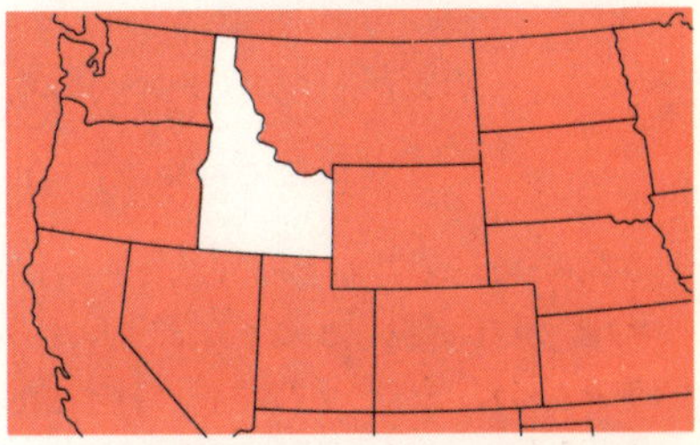

ELEVATION

High: 12,662 feet
Low: 720 feet

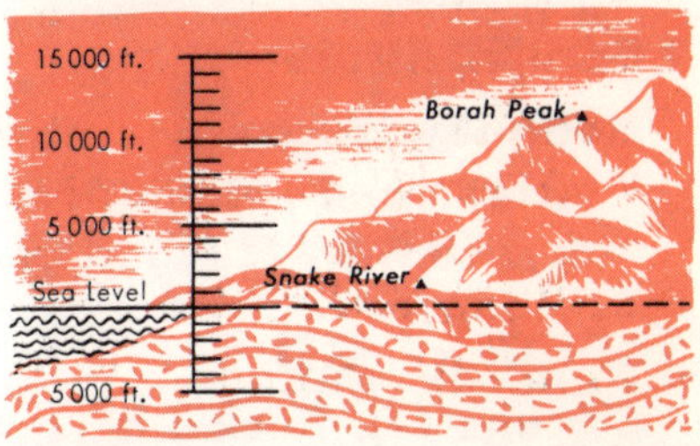

CAPITAL

Boise

ADMITTED TO UNION

1890 as 43rd state

SEAL & MOTTO

"Esto Perpetua"
("It is forever")

Illinois

NICKNAME: Land of Lincoln

Originally part of the Northwest Territory, 1787; made separate territory, 1809.

BOUNDARIES

North by Wisconsin, east by Lake Michigan and Indiana, south by Kentucky, west by Missouri and Iowa.

LARGEST CITIES

Chicago (1), Rockford (2), Peoria (3), Springfield (4), Decatur (5).

POPULATION: 11,113,976
RANK: 5th

TIME ZONE: Central

SONG: "Illinois"

BIRD

Cardinal

FLOWER

Native Violet

ORIGIN OF NAME

Indian, meaning "Tribe of Men"

DISCOVERED

1673 by Marquette and Jolliet (French)

SETTLED

1699 by the French at Cahokia

AREA & LOCATION

56,400 square miles
24th in size

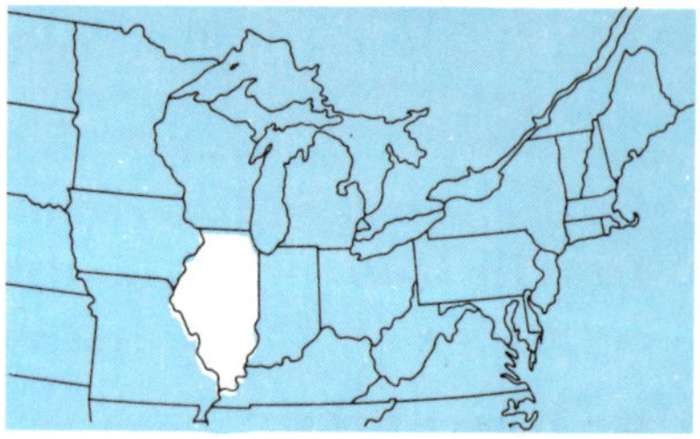

ELEVATION

High: 1,241 feet
Low: 279 feet

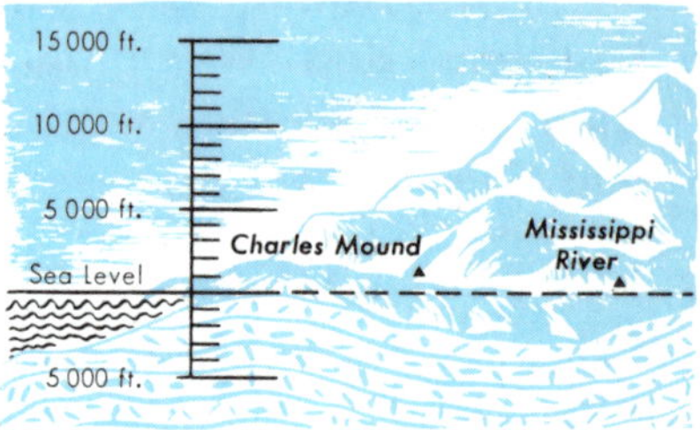

CAPITAL

Springfield

ADMITTED TO UNION

1818 as 21st state

SEAL & MOTTO

"State Sovereignty—National Union"

Indiana

NICKNAME: Hoosier State

Part of the Northwest Territory, 1787; separate territory, 1800.

BOUNDARIES
North by Lake Michigan and Michigan, east by Ohio, south by Kentucky, west by Illinois.

LARGEST CITIES
Indianapolis (1), Fort Wayne (2), Gary (3), Evansville (4), South Bend (5).

POPULATION: 5,193,669
RANK: 11th

TIME ZONE
6 NW & 6 SW counties: Central
Remainder of state: Eastern

SONG: "On the Banks of the Wabash"

BIRD

Cardinal

FLOWER

Peony

ORIGIN OF NAME
English, for "Land of Indians"

DISCOVERED
1679 by La Salle (French)

SETTLED
1732 by French at Vincennes

AREA & LOCATION
36,291 square miles
38th in size

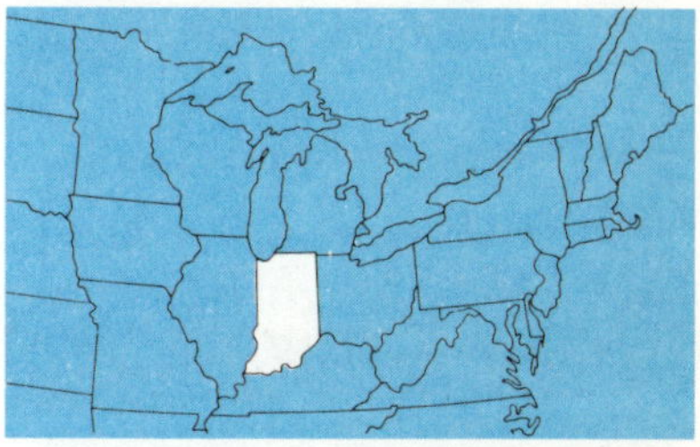

ELEVATION
High: 1,257 feet
Low: 320 feet

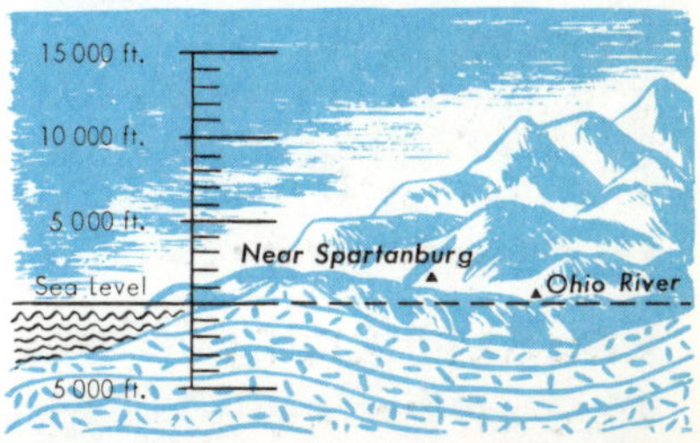

CAPITAL
Indianapolis

ADMITTED TO UNION
1816 as 19th state

SEAL & MOTTO
"The Crossroads of America"

Iowa

NICKNAME: Hawkeye State

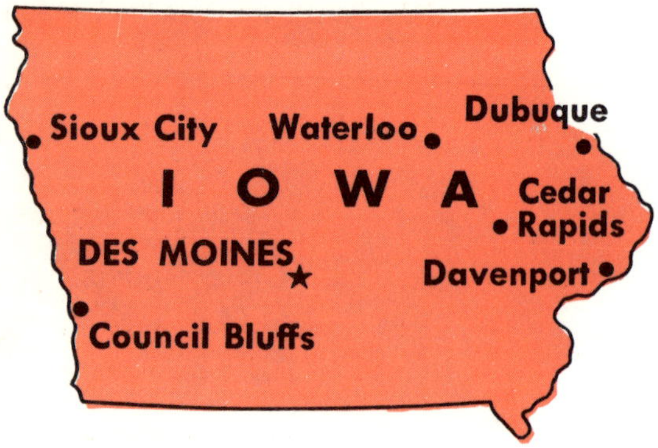

Part of the Louisiana Purchase of 1803; organized as separate territory, 1838.

BOUNDARIES

North by Minnesota, east by Wisconsin and Illinois, south by Missouri, west by Nebraska and South Dakota.

LARGEST CITIES

Des Moines (1), Cedar Rapids (2), Davenport (3), Sioux City (4), Waterloo (5), Dubuque (6), Council Bluffs (7).

POPULATION: 2,825,041
RANK: 25th

TIME ZONE: Central

SONG: "Iowa"

BIRD

Eastern Goldfinch

FLOWER

Wild Rose

ORIGIN OF NAME

Indian, probably meaning "This is the Place"

DISCOVERED

1673 by Marquette and Jolliet (French)

SETTLED

1833 by Americans at Dubuque

AREA & LOCATION

56,290 square miles
25th in size

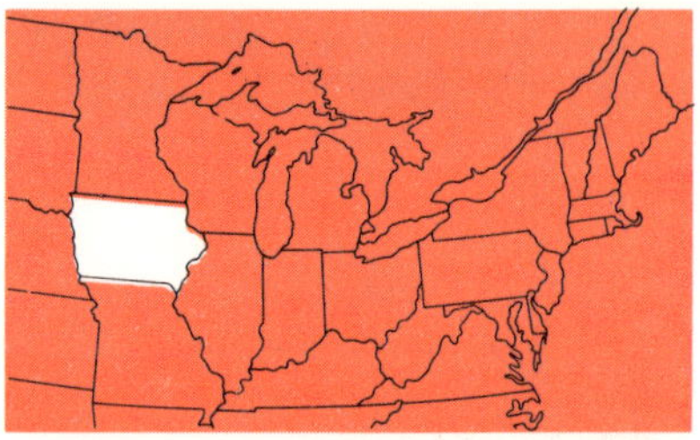

ELEVATION

High: 1,675 feet
Low: 480 feet

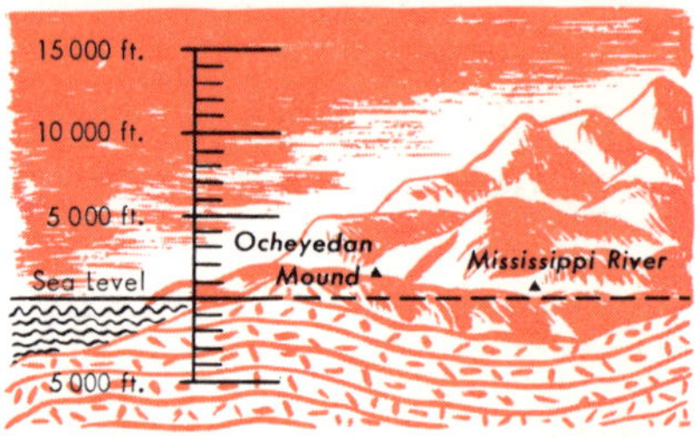

CAPITAL

Des Moines

ADMITTED TO UNION

1846 as 29th state

SEAL & MOTTO

"Our Liberties We Prize and Our Rights We Will Maintain"

Kansas

NICKNAME: Sunflower State

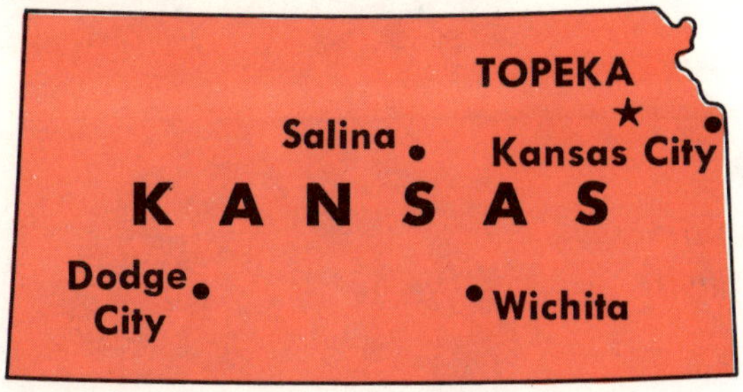

Area originally claimed by Spain and France; part of the Louisiana Purchase of 1803; made a separate territory in 1854 by the Kansas-Nebraska Act.

BOUNDARIES

On the north by Nebraska, east by Missouri, south by Oklahoma, and west by Colorado.

LARGEST CITIES

Wichita (1), Kansas City (2), Topeka (3), Overland Park (4), Lawrence (5).

POPULATION: 2,249,071
RANK: 28th

TIME ZONE

4½ western counties: Mountain
Remainder of state: Central

SONG: "Home on the Range"

BIRD

Western Meadow Lark

FLOWER

Sunflower

ORIGIN OF NAME

Indian, meaning "Swift Wind"

DISCOVERED

1541 by Coronado (Spanish)

SETTLED

1827 at Fort Leavenworth by Americans

AREA & LOCATION

82,264 square miles
14th in size

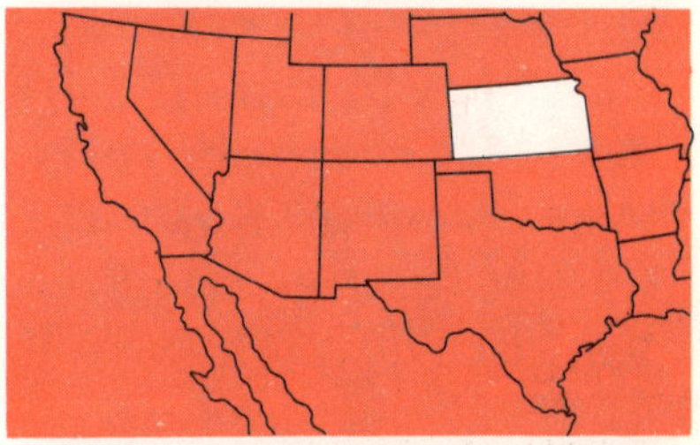

ELEVATION

High: 4,026 feet
Low: 700 feet

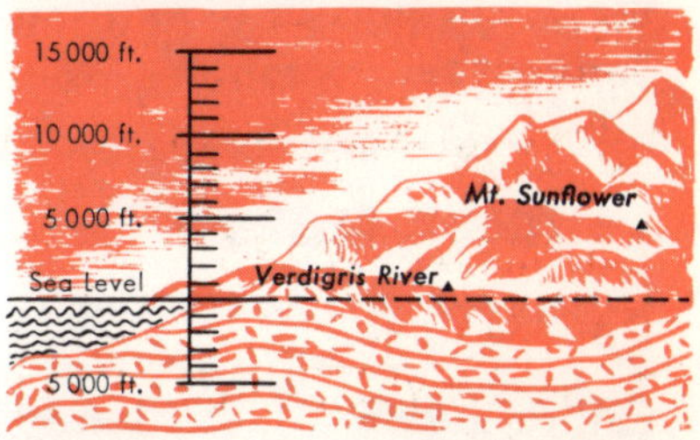

CAPITAL

Topeka

ADMITTED TO UNION

1861 as 34th state

SEAL & MOTTO

"Ad Astra per Aspera"
("To the Stars through Difficulties")

Kentucky

NICKNAME: Bluegrass State

Kentucky County formed in 1776 as part of state of Virginia; claims relinquished by Virginia in 1792. Among early pioneers were George Rogers Clark and Daniel Boone.

BOUNDARIES

North by Indiana and Ohio, east by West Virginia and Virginia, south by Tennessee, west by Missouri and Illinois.

LARGEST CITIES

Louisville (1), Lexington (2), Owensboro (3), Covington (4), Bowling Green (5), Paducah (6), Ashland (7).

POPULATION: 3,219,311
RANK: 23rd

TIME ZONE: East Half: Eastern
West Half: Central

SONG: "My Old Kentucky Home"

BIRD

Kentucky Cardinal

FLOWER

Goldenrod

ORIGIN OF NAME

Indian, meaning "Land of Tomorrow"

DISCOVERED

1673 by Marquette and Jolliet (French)

SETTLED

1774 by the English at Harrodsburg

AREA & LOCATION

40,395 square miles
37th in size

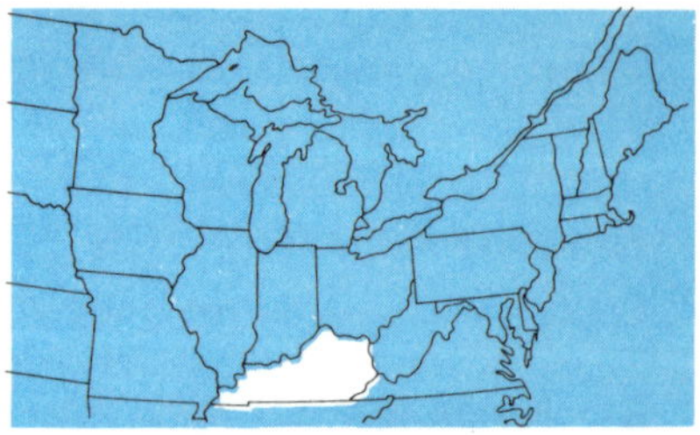

ELEVATION

High: 4,145 feet
Low: 257 feet

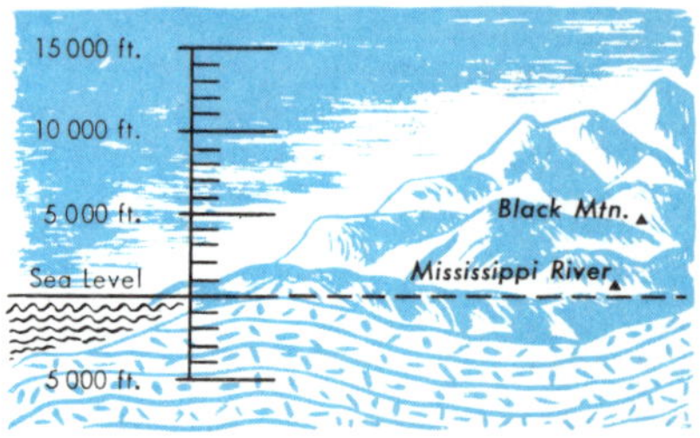

CAPITAL

Frankfort

ADMITTED TO UNION

1792 as 15th state

SEAL & MOTTO

"United We Stand, Divided We Fall"

Louisiana

NICKNAME: Pelican State

Part of the Louisiana Purchase of 1803; organized as territory in 1804.

BOUNDARIES
North by Arkansas, east by Mississippi, south by the Gulf of Mexico, west by Texas.

LARGEST CITIES
New Orleans (1), Shreveport (2), Baton Rouge (3), Metairie (4).

POPULATION: 3,643,180
RANK: 20th

TIME ZONE: Central

SONG: "Song of Louisiana"

BIRD

Eastern Brown Pelican

FLOWER

Magnolia

ORIGIN OF NAME

French, in honor of King Louis XIV

DISCOVERED

1541 by De Soto (Spanish)

SETTLED

1714 by the French at Natchitoches

AREA & LOCATION

48,523 square miles
31st in size

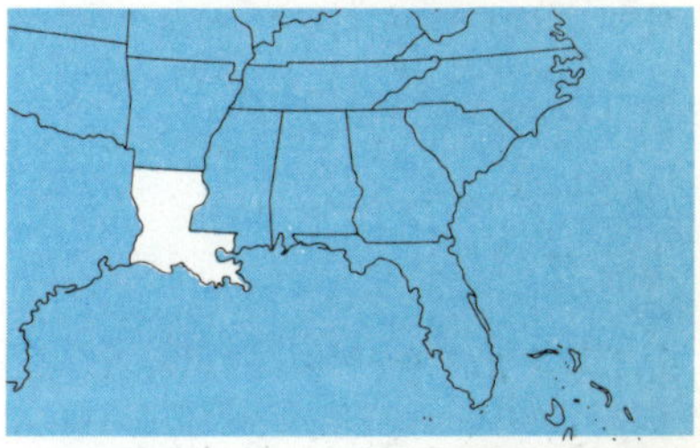

ELEVATION

High: 535 feet
Low: 5 feet below sea level

CAPITAL

Baton Rouge

ADMITTED TO UNION

1812 as 18th state

SEAL & MOTTO

"Union, Justice, Confidence"

Maine

NICKNAME: Pine Tree State

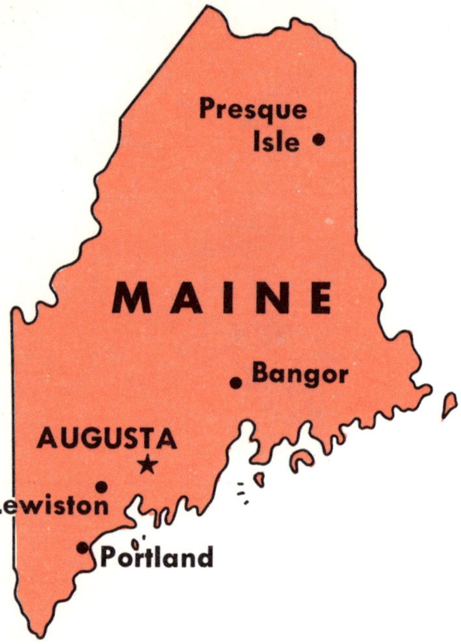

Part of land grant given to Plymouth Company in 1606 by James I; under Massachusetts jurisdiction from 1652 to 1819.

BOUNDARIES

Northwest by Quebec, northeast by New Brunswick, southeast by Atlantic Ocean, southwest by New Hampshire.

LARGEST CITIES

Portland (1), Lewiston (2), Bangor (3).

POPULATION: 993,663
RANK: 38th

TIME ZONE: Eastern

SONG: "State of Maine Song"

BIRD

Chickadee

FLOWER

White Pine Cone & Tassel

ORIGIN OF NAME

French, after province in France

DISCOVERED

1524 by Verrazano (for France)

SETTLED

1623 by the English near Saco

AREA & LOCATION

33,215 square miles
39th in size

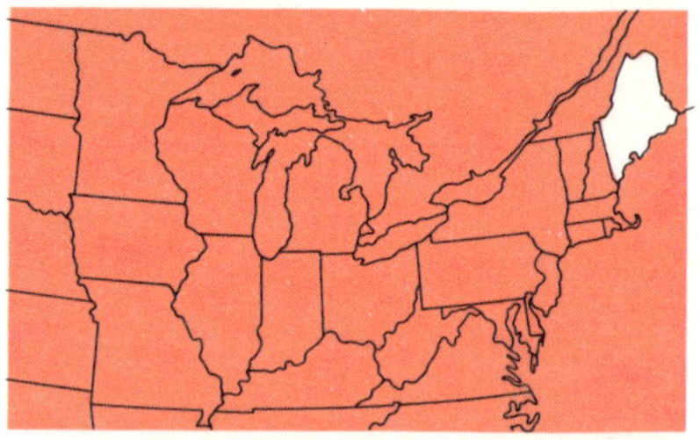

ELEVATION

High: 5,268 feet
Low: sea level

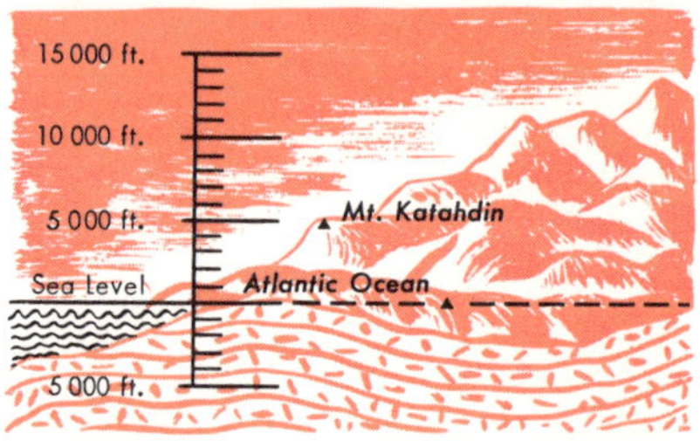

CAPITAL

Augusta

ADMITTED TO UNION

1820 as 23rd state

SEAL & MOTTO

"Dirigo" ("I Guide")

Maryland

NICKNAME: Old Line State

Charter of Maryland granted, 1632, to the second Lord Baltimore; area became royal province in 1688. Mason-Dixon Line surveyed in 1767. One of the thirteen original states.

BOUNDARIES

North by Pennsylvania, east by Delaware and the Atlantic Ocean, south by Virginia and West Virginia, west by West Virginia.

LARGEST CITIES

Baltimore (1), Dundalk (2), Silver Spring (3), Towson (4), Bethesda (5).

POPULATION: 3,922,399
RANK: 18th

TIME ZONE: Eastern

SONG: "Maryland, My Maryland"

BIRD

Baltimore Oriole

FLOWER

Black-eyed Susan

ORIGIN OF NAME

English, in honor of Queen Henrietta Maria

DISCOVERED

1608 by John Smith

SETTLED

1631 by the English on Kent Island

AREA & LOCATION

10,577 square miles
42nd in size

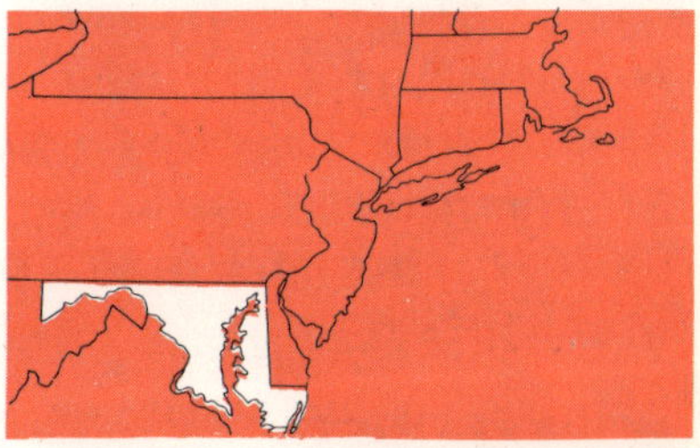

ELEVATION

High: 3,360 feet
Low: sea level

CAPITAL

Annapolis

ADMITTED TO UNION

1788 as 7th of the 13 original states

SEAL & MOTTO

"Fatti Maschii, Parole Femine" ("Manly Deeds, Womanly Words")

Massachusetts

NICKNAME: Bay State

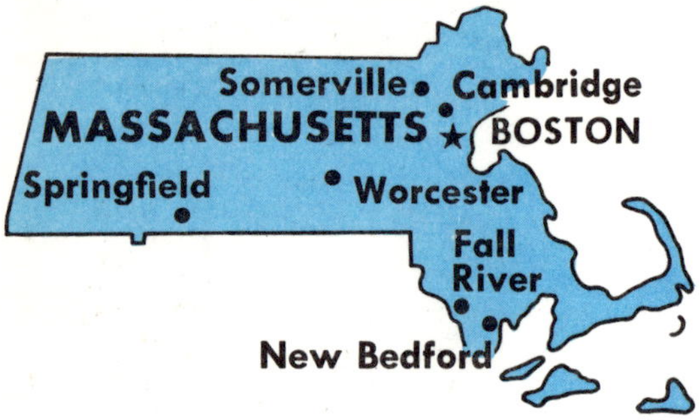

Royal charter granted in 1629 to Massachusetts Bay Company; Massachusetts made royal colony in 1691. One of the thirteen original states.

BOUNDARIES

North by Vermont and New Hampshire; east by the Atlantic Ocean; south by Connecticut, Rhode Island, and the Atlantic Ocean; west by New York.

LARGEST CITIES

Boston (1), Worcester (2), Springfield (3), New Bedford (4), Cambridge (5).

POPULATION: 5,689,170
RANK: 10th

TIME ZONE: Eastern

SONG: "Hail Massachusetts"

BIRD

Chickadee

FLOWER

Mayflower

ORIGIN OF NAME

Indian, meaning "At the Great Hill"

DISCOVERED

1602 by Bartholomew Gosnold (English)

SETTLED

1620 by English at Plymouth Rock

AREA & LOCATION

8,257 square miles
45th in size

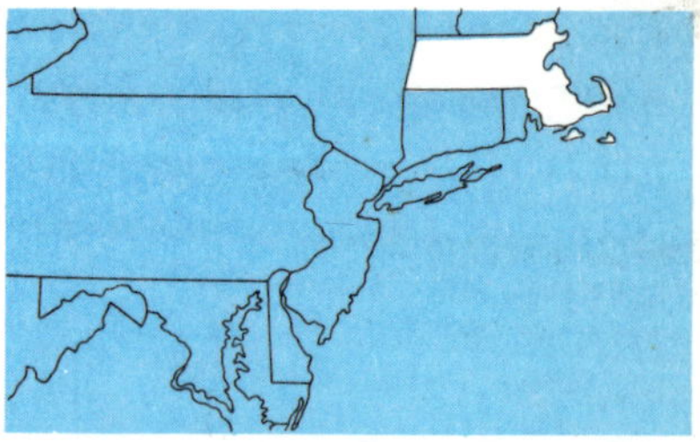

ELEVATION

High: 3,491 feet
Low: sea level

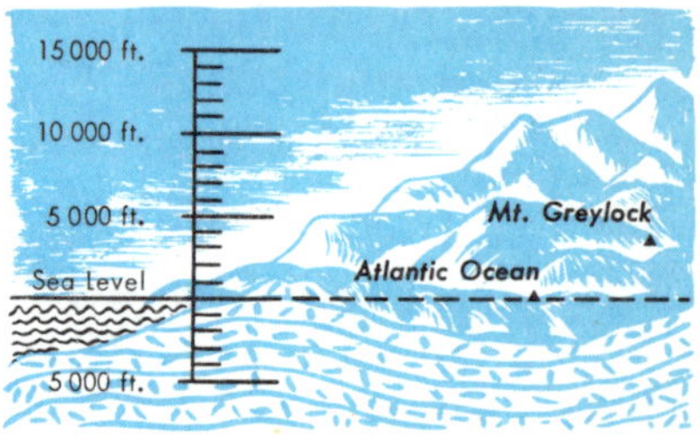

CAPITAL

Boston

ADMITTED TO UNION

1788 as 6th of the 13 original states

SEAL & MOTTO

"Ense Petit Placidam Sub Libertate Quietem" ("By the Sword We Seek Peace, but Peace Only under Liberty")

Michigan

NICKNAME: Wolverine State

Originally part of the Northwest Territory, 1787; made separate territory, 1805.

BOUNDARIES

The Upper Peninsula: north by Lake Superior, south by Wisconsin and Lake Michigan; Lower Peninsula: west by Lake Michigan, east by Lake Huron, Ontario, and Lake Erie, south by Indiana and Ohio.

LARGEST CITIES

Detroit (1), Grand Rapids (2), Flint (3), Warren (4), Lansing (5), Livonia (6).

POPULATION: 8,875,083
RANK: 7th

TIME ZONE

4 SW counties of Upper Peninsula: Central; Remainder of state: Eastern

SONG: "Michigan, My Michigan"

BIRD

Robin

FLOWER

Apple Blossom

ORIGIN OF NAME

Indian, meaning "Great Water"

DISCOVERED

1634 by Nicolet (French)

SETTLED

1668 at Sault Sainte Marie by Marquette

AREA & LOCATION

58,216 square miles
23rd in size

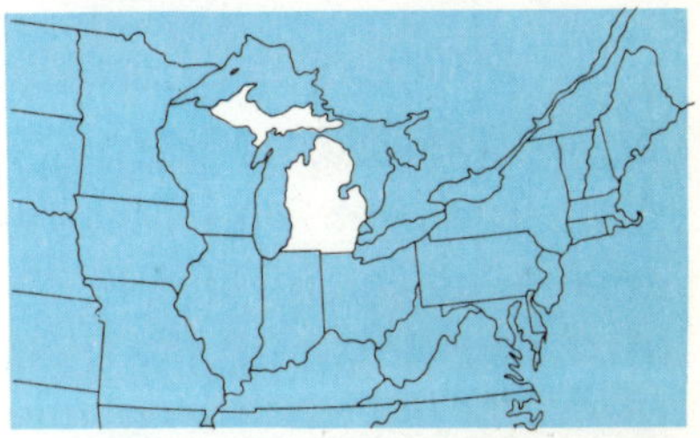

ELEVATION

High: 1,980 feet
Low: 572 feet

CAPITAL

Lansing

ADMITTED TO UNION

1837 as 26th state

SEAL & MOTTO

"Si Quaeris Peninsulam Amoenam Circumspice" ("If You Seek a Pleasant Peninsula, Look about You")

Minnesota

NICKNAME: Gopher State

Eastern section was included in Northwest Territory, 1787; western section was part of the Louisiana Purchase of 1803; Minnesota made separate territory, 1849.

BOUNDARIES

North by Manitoba and Ontario, east by Wisconsin and Lake Superior, south by Iowa, west by South Dakota and North Dakota.

LARGEST CITIES

Minneapolis (1), St. Paul (2), Duluth (3), Bloomington (4), Rochester (5).

POPULATION: 3,805,069
RANK: 19th

TIME ZONE: Central

SONG: "Hail! Minnesota"

BIRD

Loon

FLOWER

Showy Lady-Slipper

ORIGIN OF NAME

Indian, meaning "Sky-colored Water"

DISCOVERED

1655 by the French

SETTLED

Probably 1819 at Fort Snelling by Americans

AREA & LOCATION

84,068 square miles
12th in size

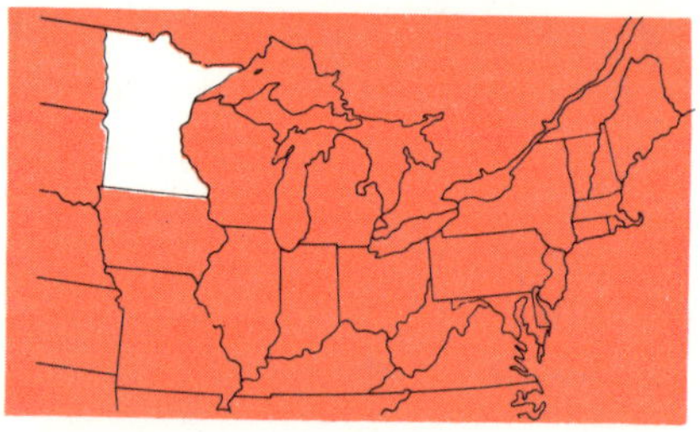

ELEVATION

High: 2,301 feet
Low: 602 feet

CAPITAL

St. Paul

ADMITTED TO UNION

1858 as 32nd state

SEAL & MOTTO

"L'etoile du Nord"
("The North Star")

Mississippi

NICKNAME: Magnolia State

Organized as territory, 1798; Georgia's claims relinquished in 1802.

BOUNDARIES

North by Tennessee, east by Alabama, south by Louisiana and the Gulf of Mexico, west by Louisiana and Arkansas.

LARGEST CITIES

Jackson (1), Biloxi (2), Meridian (3), Gulfport (4), Greenville (5).

POPULATION: 2,216,912
RANK: 29th

TIME ZONE: Central

SONG: "Go Mis-sis-sip-pi"

BIRD

Mockingbird

FLOWER

Magnolia

ORIGIN OF NAME

Indian, meaning "Great River"

DISCOVERED

1540 by De Soto (Spanish)

SETTLED

1699 on Biloxi Bay by French

AREA & LOCATION

47,716 square miles
32nd in size

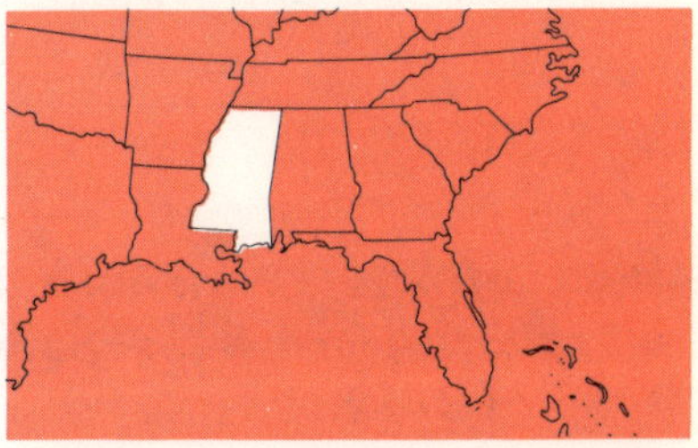

ELEVATION

High: 806 feet
Low: sea level

CAPITAL

Jackson

ADMITTED TO UNION

1817 as 20th state

SEAL & MOTTO

"Virtute et Armis"
("By Valor and Arms")

Missouri

NICKNAME: Show Me State

Part of the Louisiana Purchase of 1803; became a separate territory in 1812.

BOUNDARIES

North by Iowa; east by Illinois, Kentucky, and Tennessee; south by Arkansas; west by Oklahoma, Kansas, and Nebraska.

LARGEST CITIES

St. Louis (1), Kansas City (2), Springfield (3), Independence (4).

POPULATION: 4,677,399
RANK: 13th

TIME ZONE: Central

SONG: "Missouri Waltz"

BIRD

Bluebird

FLOWER

Hawthorne

ORIGIN OF NAME

Indian, of unknown meaning

DISCOVERED

1673 by Marquette and Jolliet (French)

SETTLED

1735 by the French at Ste. Genevieve

AREA & LOCATION

69,686 square miles
19th in size

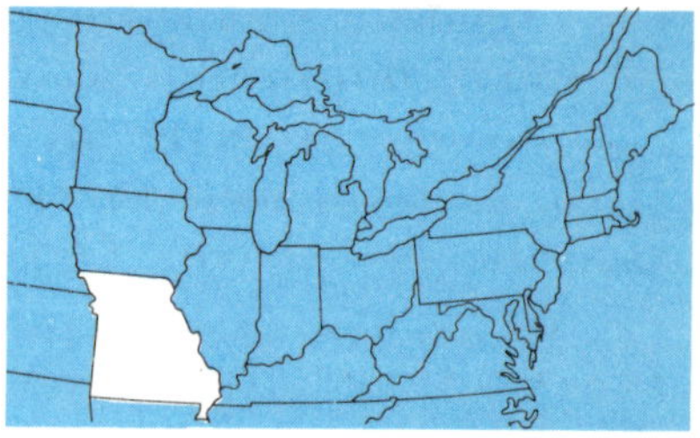

ELEVATION

High: 1,772 feet
Low: 230 feet

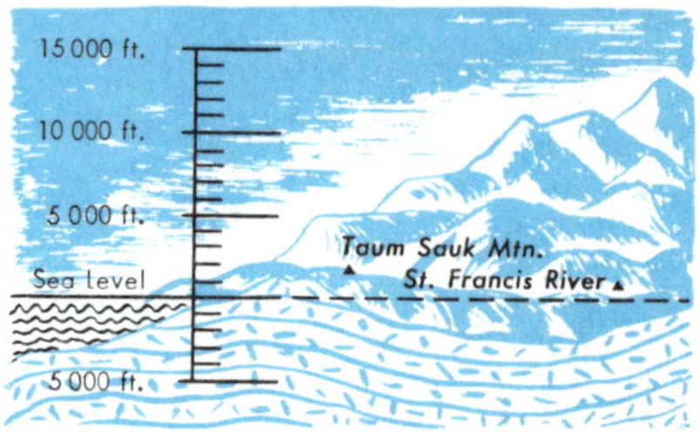

CAPITAL

Jefferson City

ADMITTED TO UNION

1821 as 24th state

SEAL & MOTTO

"Salus Populi Suprema Lex Esto" ("Let the Welfare of the People Be the Supreme Law")

Montana

NICKNAME: Treasure State

Part of the Louisiana Purchase of 1803; boundary with Canada settled by treaties in 1818 and 1846. Area formed parts of Washington, Nebraska, Dakota, and Idaho territories, until it was made a separate territory in 1864.

BOUNDARIES

North by British Columbia, Alberta, and Saskatchewan; east by North Dakota and South Dakota; south by Wyoming and Idaho; west by Idaho.

LARGEST CITIES

Billings (1), Great Falls (2), Missoula (3), Helena (4), Butte (5).

POPULATION: 694,409
RANK: 43rd

TIME ZONE: Mountain

SONG: "Montana"

BIRD

Western Meadowlark

FLOWER

Bitterroot

ORIGIN OF NAME

Latin, meaning "Mountainous Regions"

DISCOVERED

1743 by the French

SETTLED

1855 in Bitterroot Valley by Americans

AREA & LOCATION

147,138 square miles
4th in size

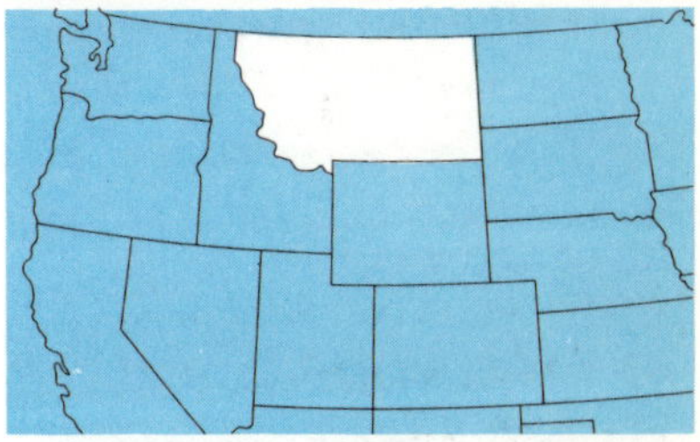

ELEVATION

High: 12,799 feet
Low: 1,800 feet

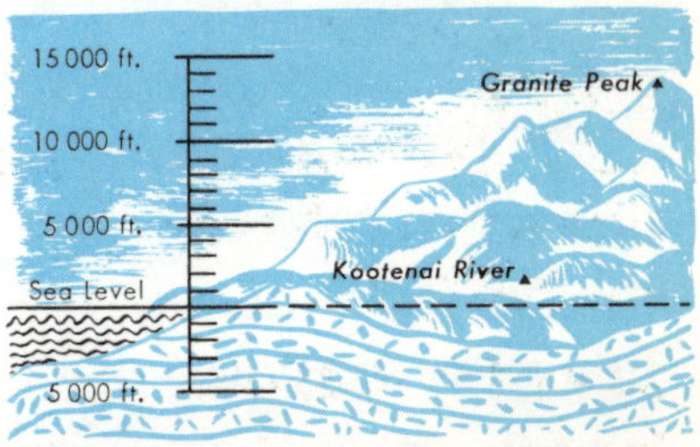

CAPITAL

Helena

ADMITTED TO UNION

1889 as 41st state

SEAL & MOTTO

"Oro y Plata" ("Gold and Silver")

Nebraska

NICKNAME: Cornhusker State

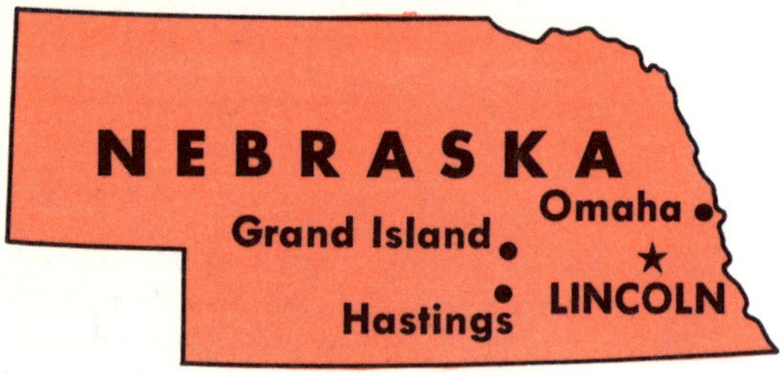

Part of the Louisiana Purchase of 1803; organized as separate territory in 1854 with passage of Kansas-Nebraska Act. Omaha served as territorial capital from 1855 to 1867.

BOUNDARIES
North by South Dakota, east by Iowa and Missouri, south by Kansas and Colorado, west by Colorado and Wyoming.

LARGEST CITIES
Omaha (1), Lincoln (2), Grand Island (3), Bellevue (4), Fremont (5).

POPULATION: 1,483,791
RANK: 35th

TIME ZONE
Eastern two-thirds: Central
Western third: Mountain

SONG: "Beautiful Nebraska"

BIRD

Western Meadowlark

FLOWER

Goldenrod

ORIGIN OF NAME
Indian, meaning "Flat Water"

DISCOVERED
1541 by Coronado (Spanish)

SETTLED
1823 at Bellevue by Americans

AREA & LOCATION
77,227 square miles
15th in size

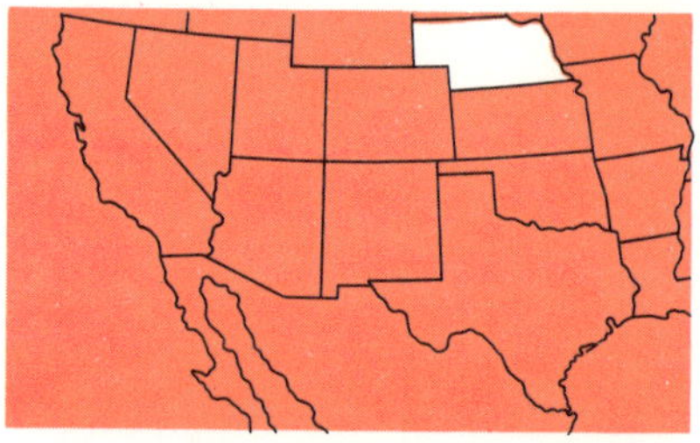

ELEVATION
High: 5,424 feet
Low: 840 feet

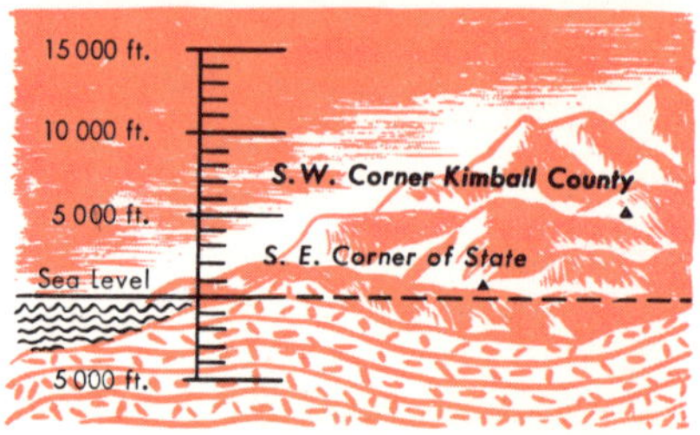

CAPITAL
Lincoln

ADMITTED TO UNION
1867 as 37th state

SEAL & MOTTO
"Equality before the Law"

Nevada

NICKNAME: Silver State

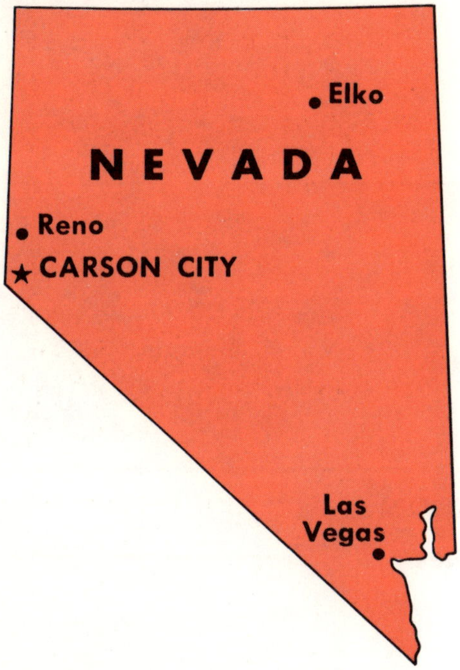

Included in Mexican Cession of 1848; part of Utah Territory, 1850; separate territory, 1861.

BOUNDARIES

North by Oregon and Idaho, east by Utah and Arizona, southwest and west by California.

LARGEST CITIES

Las Vegas (1), Reno (2).

POPULATION: 488,738
RANK: 47th

TIME ZONE: Pacific

SONG: "Home Means Nevada"

BIRD

Mountain Bluebird

FLOWER

Sagebrush

ORIGIN OF NAME

Spanish, meaning "Snow Clad"

DISCOVERED

1775 by the Spanish

SETTLED

1849 by Mormons at Genoa

AREA & LOCATION

110,540 square miles
7th in size

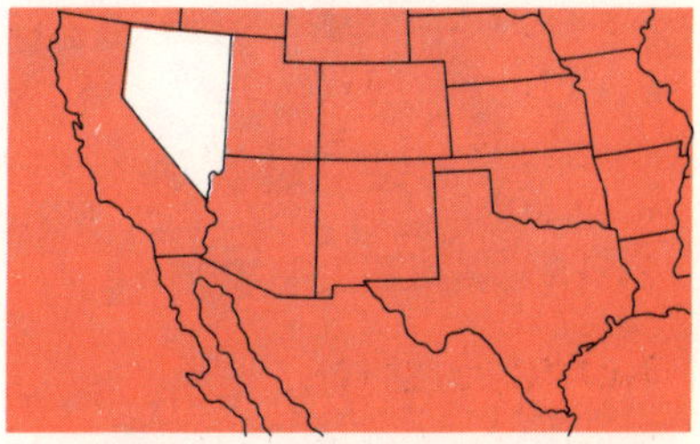

ELEVATION

High: 13,145 feet
Low: 470 feet

CAPITAL

Carson City

ADMITTED TO UNION

1864 as 36th state

SEAL & MOTTO

"All for Our Country"

New Hampshire

NICKNAME: Granite State

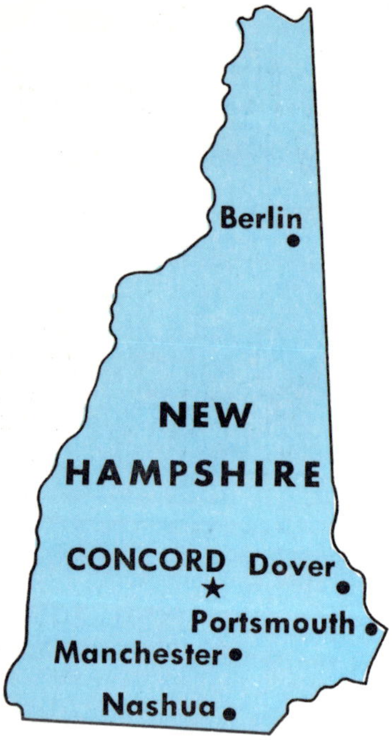

Made royal province in 1679; one of the thirteen original states.

BOUNDARIES
North by Quebec, east by Maine and the Atlantic Ocean, south by Massachusetts, west by Vermont.

LARGEST CITIES
Manchester (1), Nashua (2), Concord (3), Portsmouth (4), Dover (5).

POPULATION: 737,681
RANK: 41st

TIME ZONE: Eastern

SONG: "Old New Hampshire"

BIRD

Purple Finch

FLOWER

Purple Lilac

ORIGIN OF NAME

English, after Hampshire County, England

DISCOVERED

1603 by the English

SETTLED

1623 by the English at Dover

AREA & LOCATION

9,304 square miles
44th in size

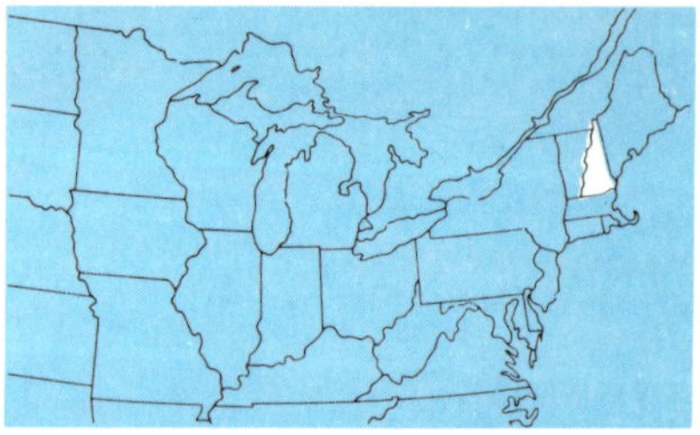

ELEVATION

High: 6,288 feet
Low: sea level

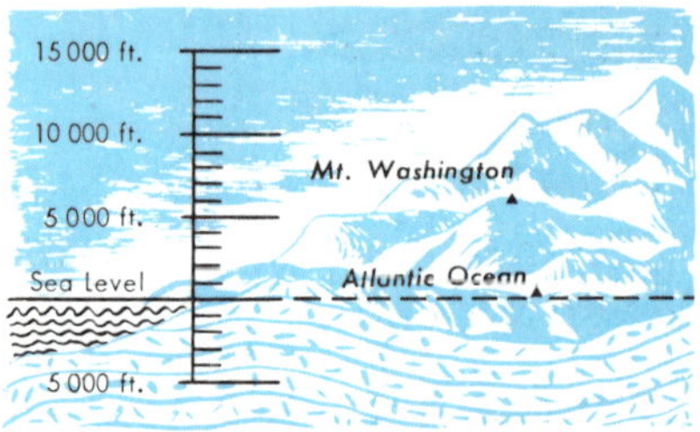

CAPITAL

Concord

ADMITTED TO UNION

1788 as 9th of the 13 original states

SEAL & MOTTO

"Live Free or Die"

New Jersey

NICKNAME: Garden State

Area granted in 1664 to Berkeley and Carteret; made royal province, 1702; one of the thirteen original states

BOUNDARIES

North by New York, east by New York and the Atlantic Ocean, south by Delaware Bay, west by Delaware and Pennsylvania.

LARGEST CITIES

Newark (1), Jersey City (2), Paterson (3), Elizabeth (4), Trenton (5), Camden (6), Clifton (7).

POPULATION: 7,168,164
RANK: 8th

TIME ZONE: Eastern

BIRD

Eastern Goldfinch

FLOWER

Purple Violet

ORIGIN OF NAME

English, after Channel Island of Jersey

DISCOVERED

1524 by Verrazano (for France)

SETTLED

1618 by the Dutch at Bergen

AREA & LOCATION

7,836 square miles
46th in size

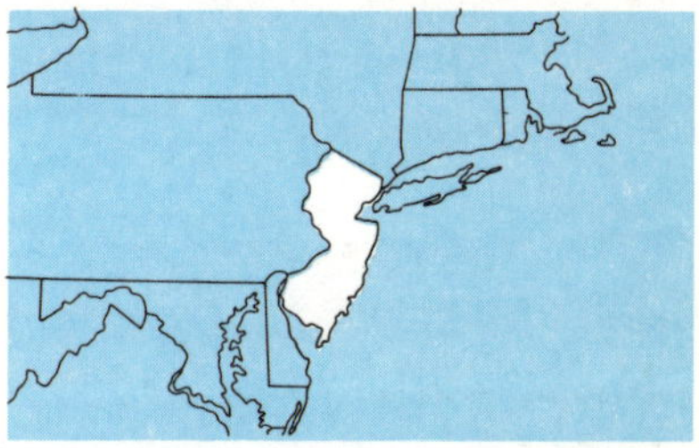

ELEVATION

High: 1,803 feet
Low: sea level

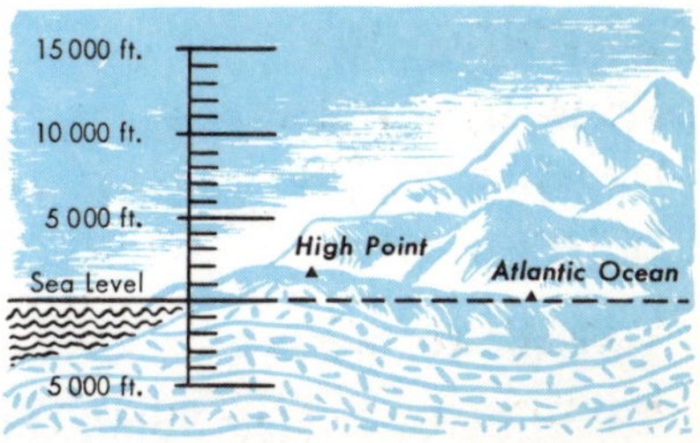

CAPITAL

Trenton

ADMITTED TO UNION

1787 as 3rd of the 13 original states

SEAL & MOTTO

"Liberty and Prosperity"

New Mexico

NICKNAME: Land of Enchantment

Part of the Mexican Cession of 1848; made territory in 1850.

BOUNDARIES

North by Colorado, east by Oklahoma and Texas, south by Texas and Mexico, west by Arizona.

LARGEST CITIES

Albuquerque (1), Santa Fe (2), Las Cruces (3), Roswell (4).

POPULATION: 1,016,000
RANK: 37th

TIME ZONE: Mountain

SONG: "O Fair New Mexico"

BIRD

Road Runner

FLOWER

Yucca

ORIGIN OF NAME

Indian, after Aztec War God

DISCOVERED

1539 by the Spanish

SETTLED

1598 by the Spanish at San Juan

AREA & LOCATION

121,666 square miles
5th in size

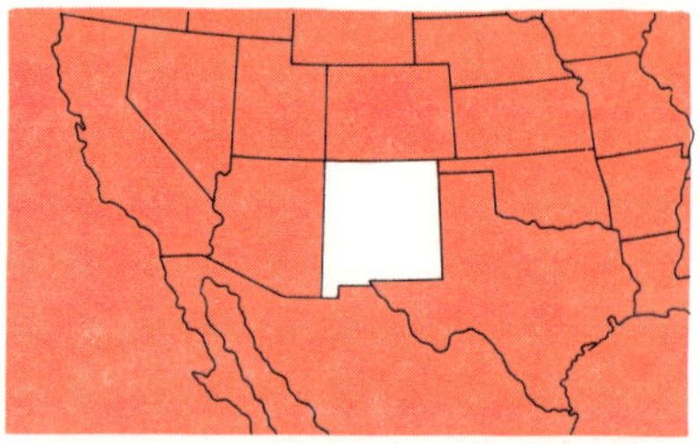

ELEVATION

High: 13,160 feet
Low: 2,817 feet

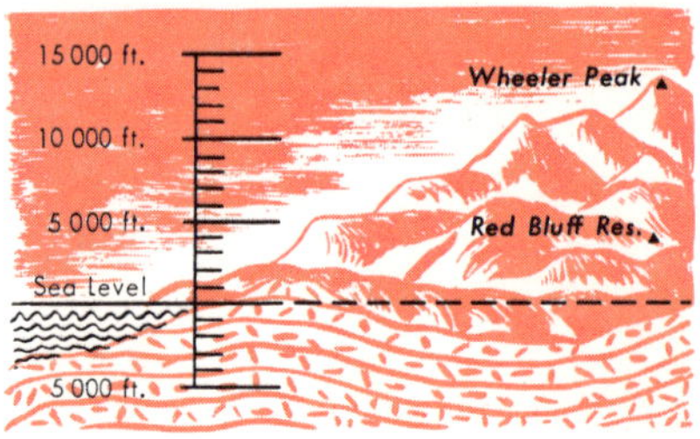

CAPITAL

Santa Fe

ADMITTED TO UNION

1912 as 47th state

SEAL & MOTTO

"Crescit Eundo"
("We Grow as We Go")

New York

NICKNAME: Empire State

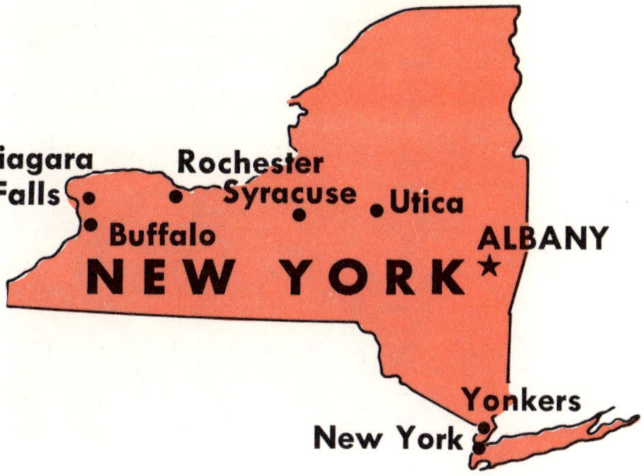

Dutch New Netherland colony surrendered to English in 1664; renamed New York; one of the thirteen original states.

BOUNDARIES

North by Lake Ontario, Ontario, and Quebec; east by Vermont, Massachusetts, and Connecticut; south by the Atlantic Ocean, New Jersey, and Pennsylvania; west by Lake Erie and Ontario.

LARGEST CITIES

New York (1), Buffalo (2), Rochester (3), Yonkers (4), Syracuse (5), Albany (6), Cheektowaga (7).

POPULATION: 18,241,266
RANK: 2nd

TIME ZONE: Eastern

BIRD

Bluebird

FLOWER

Rose

ORIGIN OF NAME

English, in honor of the Duke of York

DISCOVERED

1524 by Verrazano (for France)

SETTLED

1624 by the Dutch at Fort Orange

AREA & LOCATION

49,576 square miles
30th in size

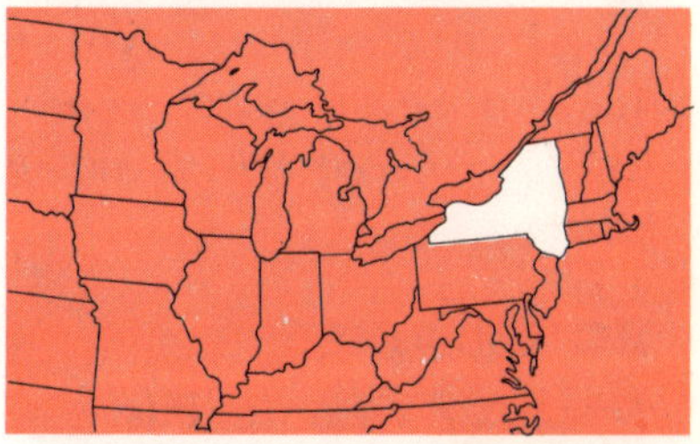

ELEVATION

High: 5,344 feet
Low: sea level

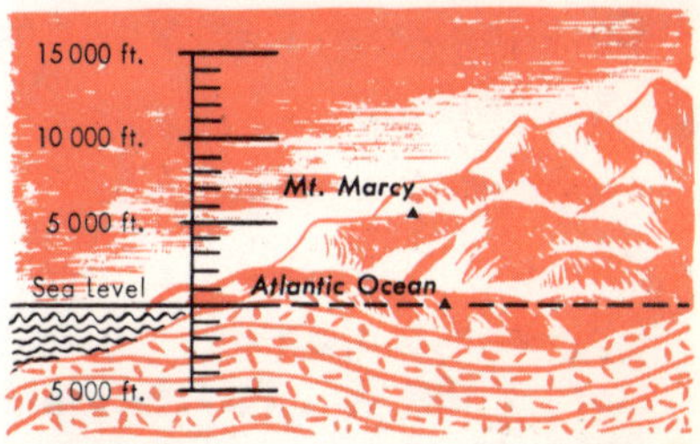

CAPITAL

Albany

ADMITTED TO UNION

1788 as 11th of the 13 original states

COAT OF ARMS & MOTTO

"Excelsior!" ("Higher!")

North Carolina

NICKNAME: Tar Heel State

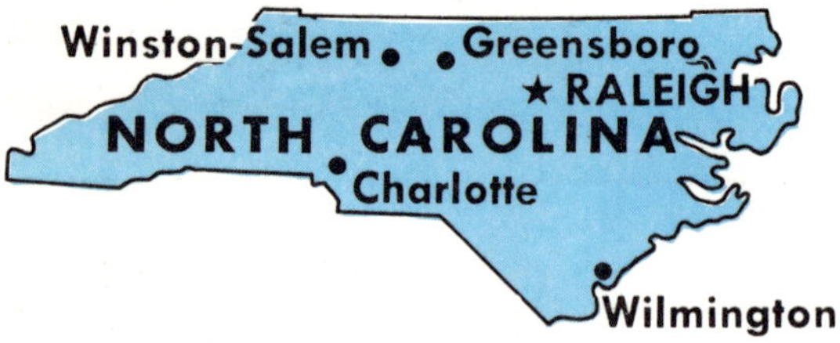

Colonists sent by Sir Walter Raleigh landed on Roanoke Island in 1585, but did not make permanent settlement. North Carolina was made royal colony in 1729; it was one of the thirteen original states.

BOUNDARIES

North by Virginia, east and southeast by the Atlantic Ocean, south by South Carolina and Georgia, and west by Tennessee.

LARGEST CITIES

Charlotte (1), Greensboro (2), Raleigh (3), Winston-Salem (4), Durham (5), High Point (6), Fayetteville (7), Asheville (8), Gastonia (9).

POPULATION: 5,082,059
RANK: 12th

TIME ZONE: Eastern

SONG: "The Old North State"

BIRD

Cardinal

FLOWER

Dogwood

ORIGIN OF NAME

English, in honor of King Charles I

DISCOVERED

1524 by Verrazano (for France)

SETTLED

1660 by the English at Albemarle Sound

AREA & LOCATION

52,712 square miles
28th in size

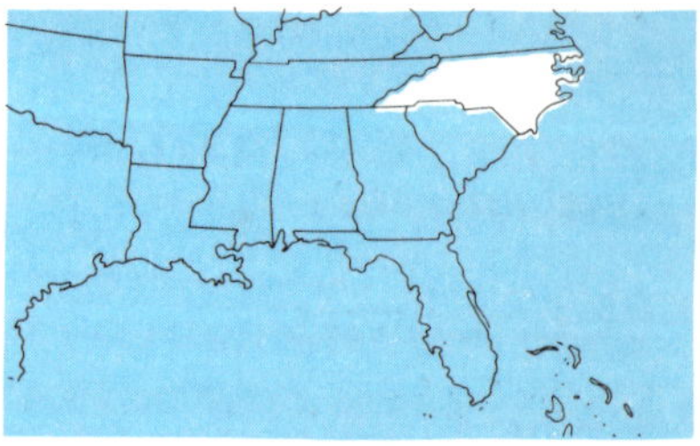

ELEVATION

High: 6,684 feet
Low: sea level

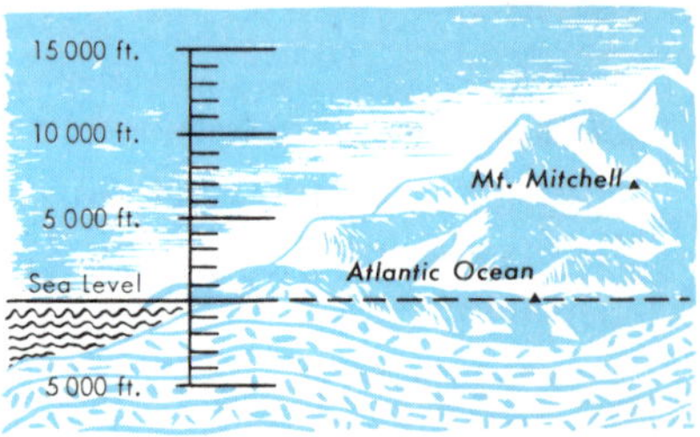

CAPITAL

Raleigh

ADMITTED TO UNION

1789 as 12th of the 13 original states

SEAL & MOTTO

"Esse Quam Videri" ("To Be Rather Than to Seem")

North Dakota

NICKNAME: Flickertail State

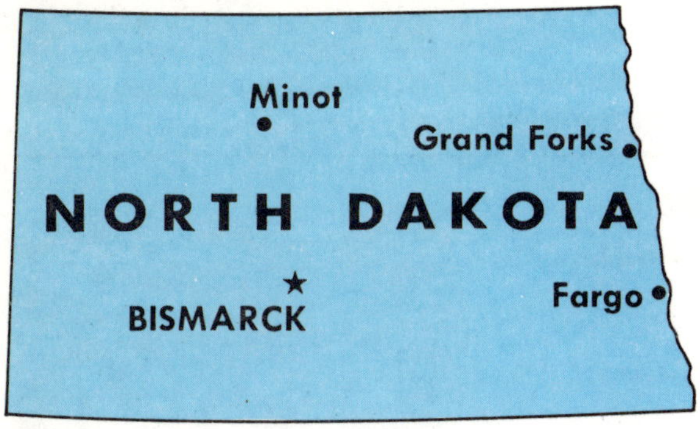

Western half was part of the Louisiana Purchase of 1803; eastern half was ceded by England in 1818; Dakota Territory organized in 1861.

BOUNDARIES

North by Saskatchewan and Manitoba, east by Minnesota, south by South Dakota, west by Montana.

LARGEST CITIES

Fargo (1), Grand Forks (2), Bismarck (3), Minot (4), Jamestown (5).

POPULATION: 617,761
RANK: 45th

TIME ZONE

One quarter (southwest): Mountain
Remainder of state: Central

SONG: "North Dakota Hymn"

BIRD

Western Meadowlark

FLOWER

Wild Prairie Rose

ORIGIN OF NAME

Indian, meaning "Alliance of Friends"

DISCOVERED

1738 by the French

SETTLED

1812 by Americans at Pembina

AREA & LOCATION

70,665 square miles
17th in size

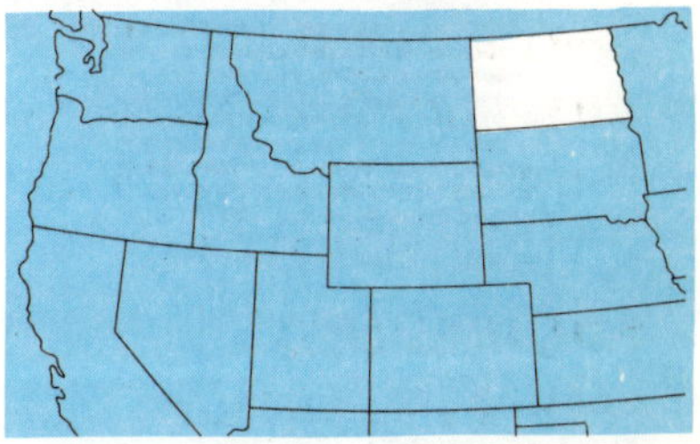

ELEVATION

High: 3,506 feet
Low: 750 feet

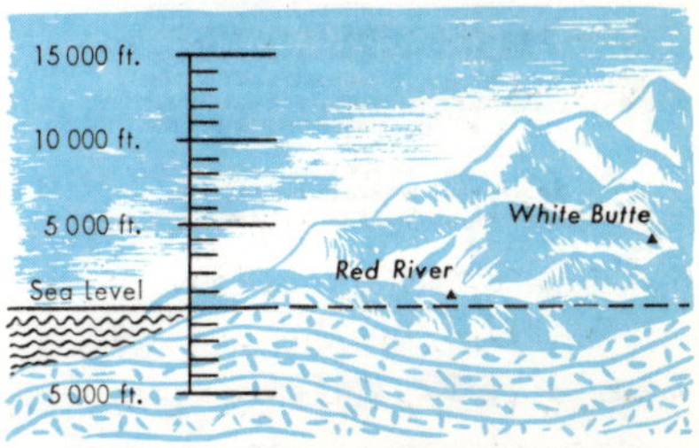

CAPITAL

Bismarck

ADMITTED TO UNION

1889 as 39th state

SEAL & MOTTO

"Liberty and Union, Now and Forever, One and Inseparable"

Ohio

NICKNAME: Buckeye State

Originally part of the Northwest Territory, 1787; organized in 1800 as separate territory.

BOUNDARIES
North by Michigan and Lake Erie, northeast by Pennsylvania, southeast by West Virginia, southwest by Kentucky, west by Indiana.

LARGEST CITIES
Cleveland (1), Columbus (2), Cincinnati (3), Toledo (4), Akron (5).

POPULATION: 10,652,017
RANK: 6th

TIME ZONE: Eastern

SONG: "Beautiful Ohio"

BIRD

Cardinal

FLOWER

Scarlet Carnation

ORIGIN OF NAME
Indian, meaning "Great River"

DISCOVERED
1670 by the French

SETTLED
1788 by Americans at Marietta

AREA & LOCATION
41,222 square miles
35th in size

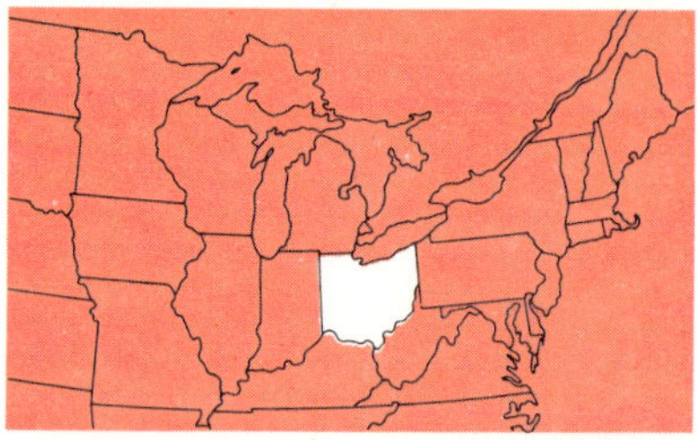

ELEVATION
High: 1,550 feet
Low: 433 feet

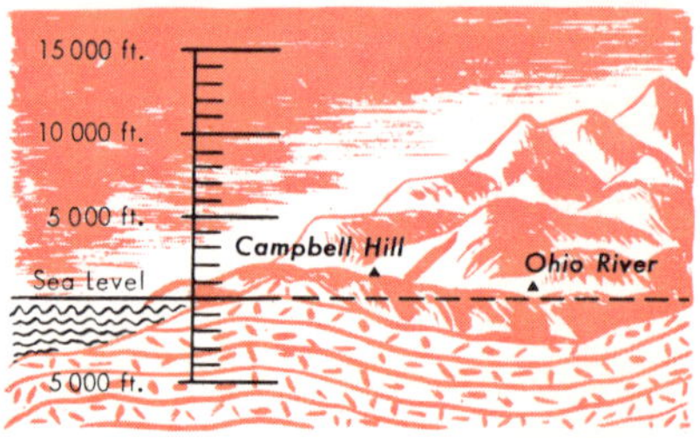

CAPITAL
Columbus

ADMITTED TO UNION
1803 as 17th state

SEAL & MOTTO
"With God, All Things Are Possible"

Oklahoma

NICKNAME: Sooner State

Part of the Louisiana Purchase of 1803; included Indian Territory and, after 1890, Oklahoma Territory.

BOUNDARIES

North by Colorado and Kansas, east by Missouri and Arkansas, south by Texas, and west by Texas and New Mexico.

LARGEST CITIES

Oklahoma City (1), Tulsa (2), Lawton (3), Norman (4), Midwest City (5).

POPULATION: 2,559,253
RANK: 27th

TIME ZONE: Central

SONG: "Oklahoma"

BIRD

Scissor-tailed Flycatcher

FLOWER

Mistletoe

ORIGIN OF NAME

Indian, meaning "Red People"

DISCOVERED

1541 by Coronado (Spanish)

SETTLED

About 1802 by the French at Salina

AREA & LOCATION

69,919 square miles
18th in size

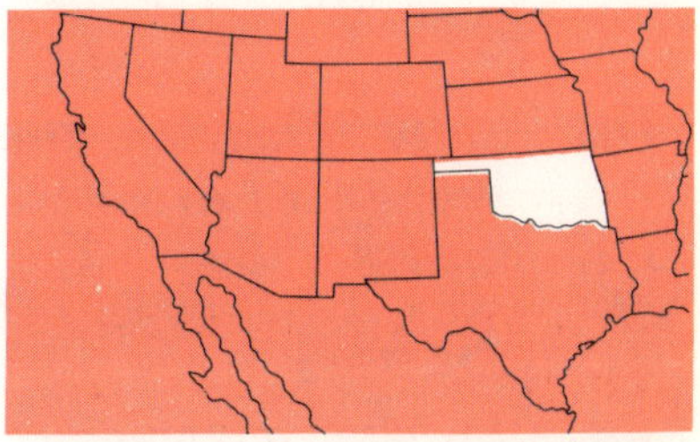

ELEVATION

High: 4,978 feet
Low: 300 feet

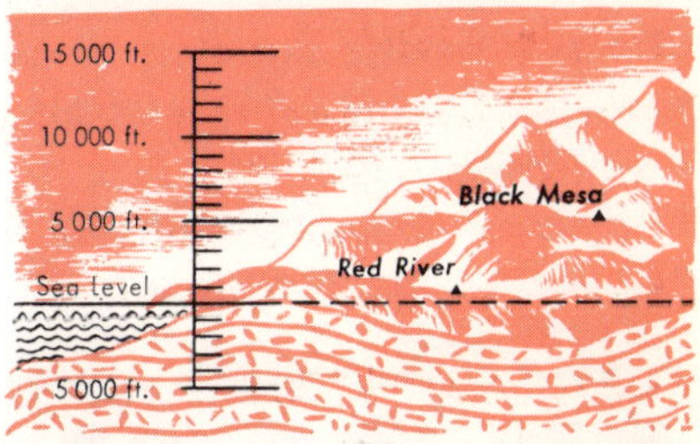

CAPITAL

Oklahoma City

ADMITTED TO UNION

1907 as 46th state

SEAL & MOTTO

"Labor Omnia Vincit" ("Labor Conquers All Things")

Oregon

NICKNAME: Beaver State

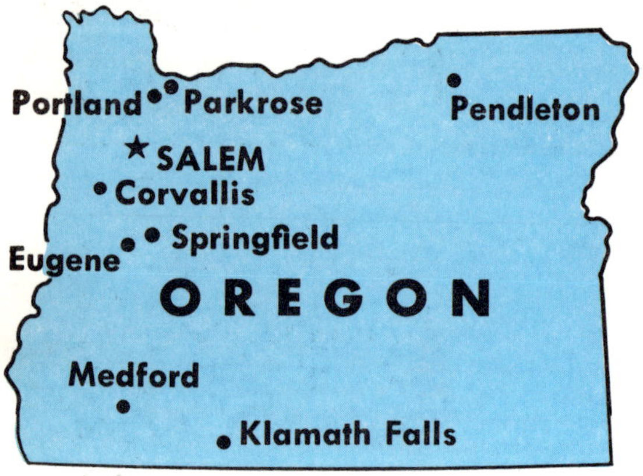

Originally part of the Oregon Country, 1846; organized as territory, 1848.

BOUNDARIES
North by Washington, east by Idaho, south by Nevada and California, west by the Pacific Ocean.

LARGEST CITIES
Portland (1), Eugene (2), Salem (3), Corvallis (4), Springfield (5), Medford (6), Parkrose (7).

POPULATION: 2,091,385
RANK: 31st

TIME ZONE
Part of Malheur County: Mountain
Remainder of state: Pacific

SONG: "Oregon, My Oregon"

BIRD

Western Meadowlark

FLOWER

Oregon Grape

ORIGIN OF NAME
Indian, meaning uncertain

DISCOVERED
1543 by the Spanish

SETTLED
1811 by Americans at Astoria

AREA & LOCATION
96,981 square miles
10th in size

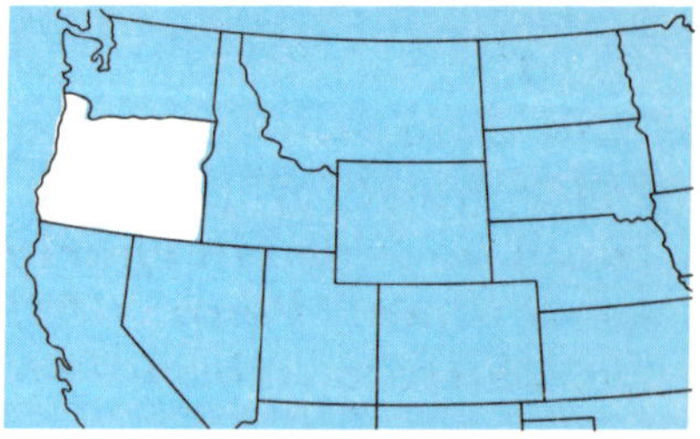

ELEVATION
High: 11,245 feet
Low: sea level

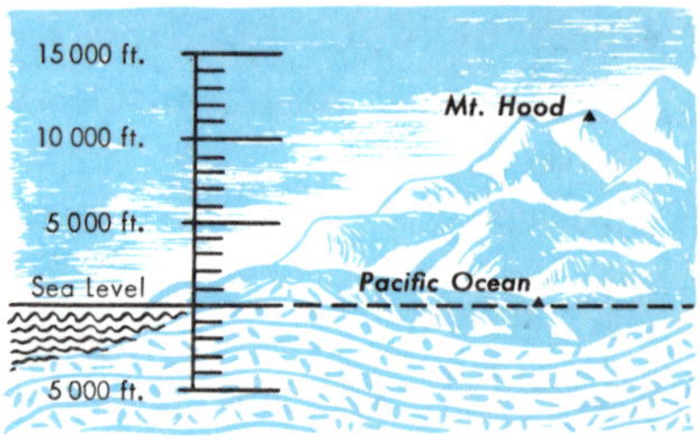

CAPITAL
Salem

ADMITTED TO UNION
1859 as 33rd state

SEAL & MOTTO
"The Union"

Pennsylvania

NICKNAME: Keystone State

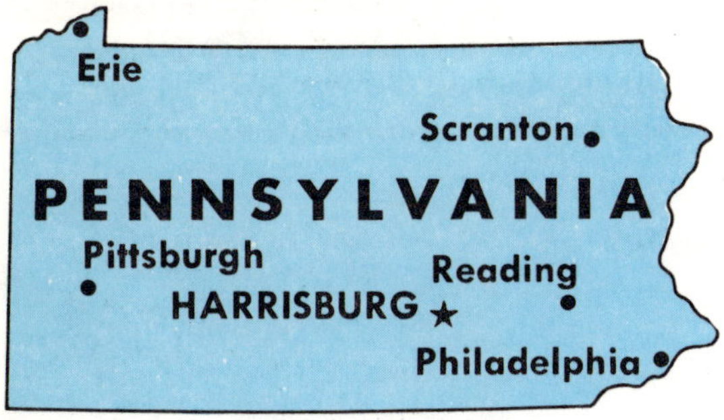

Swedish settlement at Tinicum Island taken over by the Dutch in 1655; most of present Pennsylvania included in charter granted to William Penn, 1681; one of the thirteen original states.

BOUNDARIES

North by Lake Erie and New York; east by New York and New Jersey; south by Delaware, Maryland, and West Virginia; west by West Virginia and Ohio.

LARGEST CITIES

Philadelphia (1), Pittsburgh (2), Erie (3), Allentown (4), Scranton (5), Reading (6), Levittown (7).

POPULATION: 11,793,909
RANK: 3rd

TIME ZONE: Eastern

BIRD

Ruffed Grouse

FLOWER

Mountain Laurel

ORIGIN OF NAME

English, in honor of Wm. Penn

DISCOVERED

1609 by Henry Hudson (Dutch)

SETTLED

1643 by Swedes on Tinicum Island

AREA & LOCATION

45,333 square miles
33rd in size

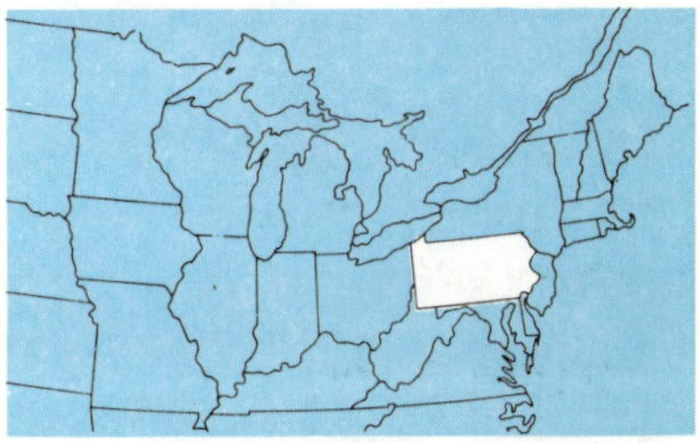

ELEVATION

High: 3,213 feet
Low: sea level

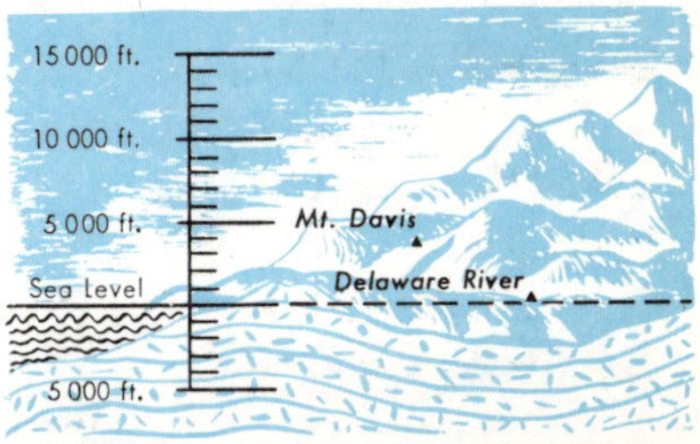

CAPITAL

Harrisburg

ADMITTED TO UNION

1787 as 2nd of the 13 original states

SEAL & MOTTO

"Virtue, Liberty and Independence"

Rhode Island

NICKNAME: Little Rhody

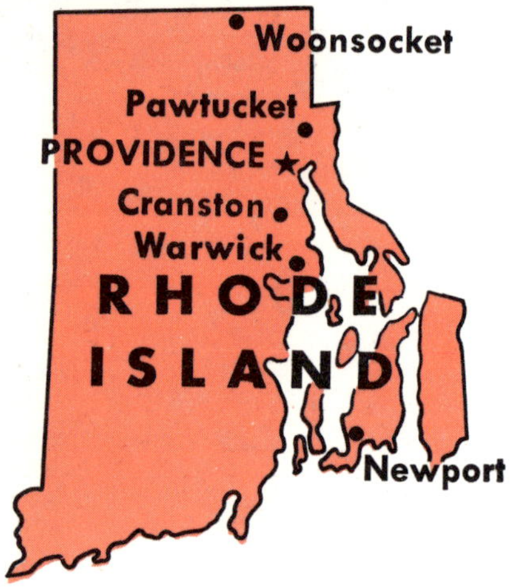

The Colony of Rhode Island and Providence Plantations granted royal charter, 1663; one of the thirteen original states.

BOUNDARIES

North and east by Massachusetts, south by the Atlantic Ocean, west by Connecticut.

LARGEST CITIES

Providence (1), Warwick (2), Cranston (3), Pawtucket (4).

POPULATION: 949,723
RANK: 39th

TIME ZONE: Eastern

SONG: "Rhode Island"

BIRD

Rhode Island Red

FLOWER

Violet

ORIGIN OF NAME

Greek, after Island of Rhodes (Island of Roses)

DISCOVERED

1524 by Verrazano (for France)

SETTLED

1636 by English at Providence

AREA & LOCATION

1,214 square miles
50th in size

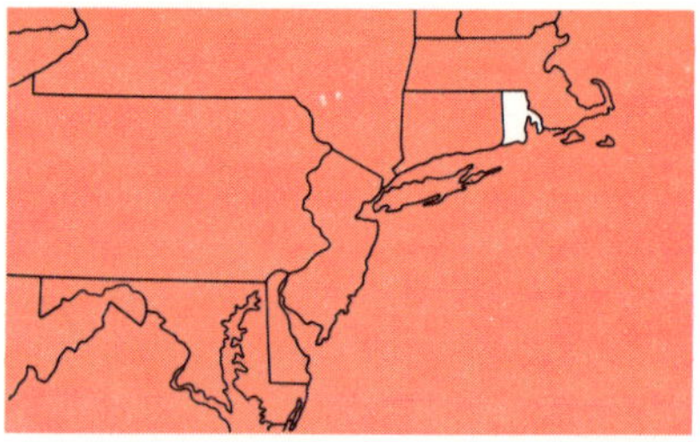

ELEVATION

High: 812 feet
Low: sea level

CAPITAL

Providence

ADMITTED TO UNION

1790 as 13th of the 13 original states

SEAL & MOTTO

"Hope"

South Carolina

NICKNAME: Palmetto State

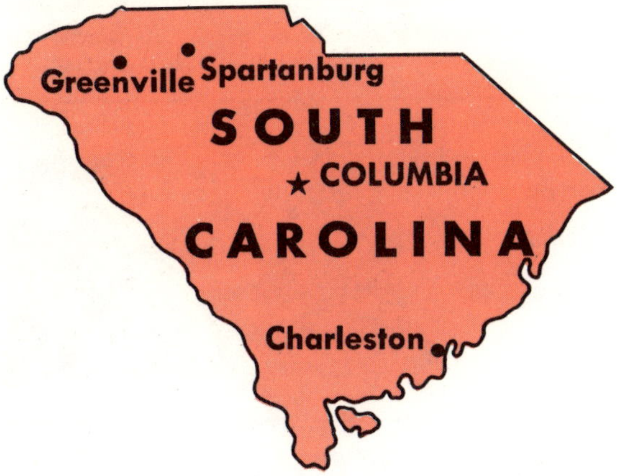

Proclaimed a royal province in 1621; one of the thirteen original states.

BOUNDARIES
North by North Carolina, southeast by the Atlantic Ocean, southwest by Georgia.

LARGEST CITIES
Columbia (1), Charleston (2), Greenville (3), Spartanburg (4).

POPULATION: 2,590,516
RANK: 26th

TIME ZONE: Eastern

SONG: "Carolina"

BIRD

Carolina Wren

FLOWER

Yellow Jessamine

ORIGIN OF NAME
English, in honor of King Charles I

DISCOVERED
1521 by the Spanish

SETTLED
1670 by the English at Charleston

AREA & LOCATION
31,055 square miles
40th in size

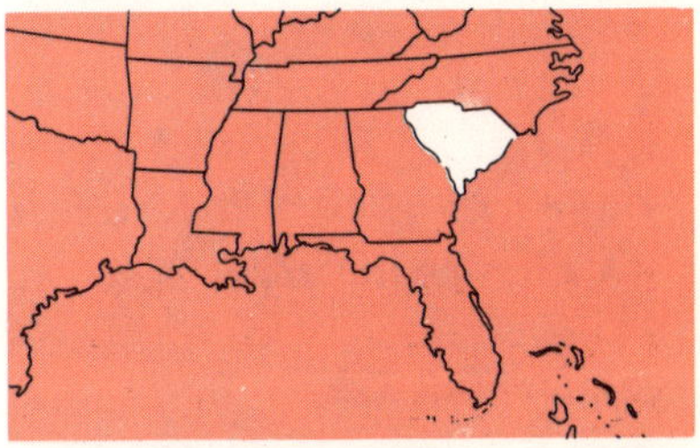

ELEVATION
High: 3,560 feet
Low: sea level

CAPITAL
Columbia

ADMITTED TO UNION
1788 as 8th of the 13 original states

SEAL & MOTTO
"Dum Spiro Spero" ("While I Breathe I Hope") and "Animis Opibusque Parati" ("Prepared in Minds and Resources")

South Dakota

NICKNAME: Coyote State

Part of the Louisiana Purchase of 1803. Dakota Territory was organized in 1861, with Yankton as the capital.

BOUNDARIES
North by North Dakota, east by Minnesota and Iowa, south by Nebraska, west by Wyoming and Montana.

LARGEST CITIES
Sioux Falls (1), Rapid City (2), Aberdeen (3).

POPULATION: 666,257
RANK: 44th

TIME ZONE
Eastern half: Central
Western half: Mountain

SONG: "Hail, South Dakota"

BIRD

Ringnecked Pheasant

FLOWER

American Pasque Flower

ORIGIN OF NAME
Indian, meaning "Alliance of Friends"

DISCOVERED
1743 by the French

SETTLED
1817 by Americans at Fort Pierre

AREA & LOCATION
77,047 square miles
16th in size

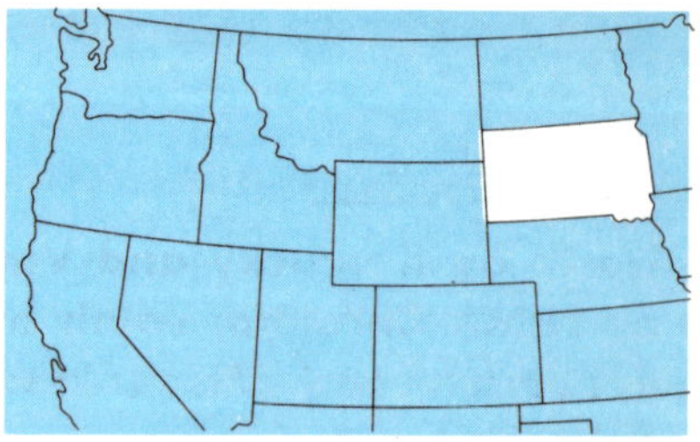

ELEVATION
High: 7,242 feet
Low: 962 feet

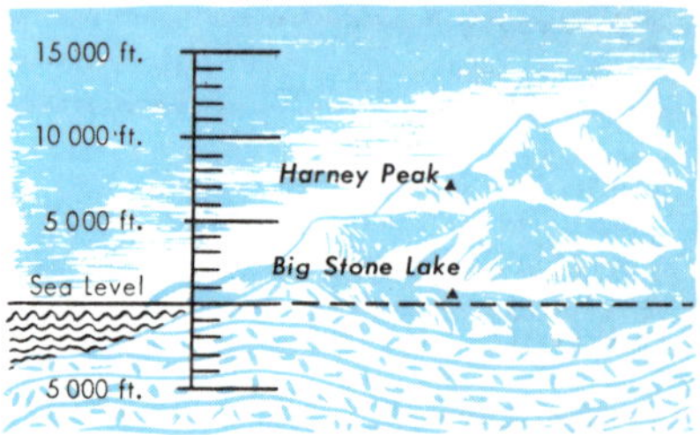

CAPITAL
Pierre

ADMITTED TO UNION
1889 as 40th state

SEAL & MOTTO
"Under God the People Rule"

Tennessee

NICKNAME: Volunteer State

Eastern section visited by De Soto in 1540; western section, by La Salle about 1682. East Tennessee formed part of independent state of Franklin in 1784–88; whole area ceded to the United States by North Carolina in 1790.

BOUNDARIES

North by Kentucky and Virginia; east by North Carolina; south by Georgia, Alabama, and Mississippi; west by Arkansas and Missouri.

LARGEST CITIES

Memphis (1), Nashville (2), Knoxville (3), Chattanooga (4).

POPULATION: 3,924,164
RANK: 17th

TIME ZONE

Eastern quarter: Eastern
Remainder of state: Central

SONG

"The Tennessee Waltz"
and
"When It's Iris Time in Tennessee"

BIRD

Mockingbird

FLOWER

Iris

ORIGIN OF NAME

Indian, meaning unknown

DISCOVERED

1540 by De Soto (Spanish)

SETTLED

1769 by the English in Watauga Valley

AREA & LOCATION

42,244 square miles
34th in size

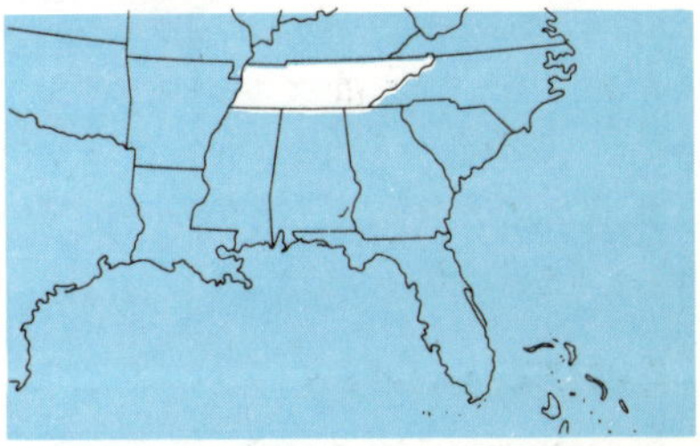

ELEVATION

High: 6,642 feet
Low: 182 feet

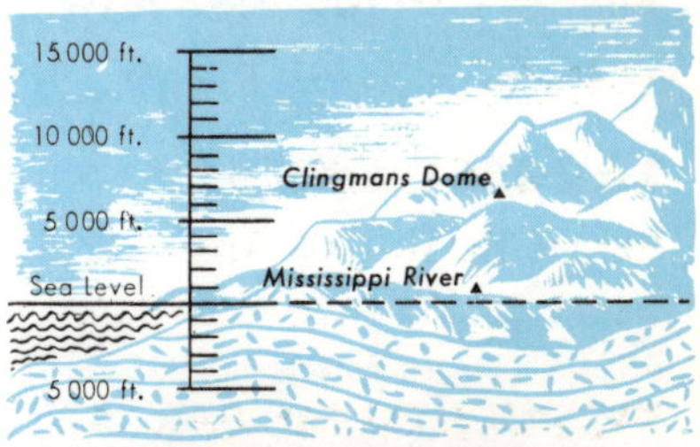

CAPITAL

Nashville

ADMITTED TO UNION

1796 as 16th state

SEAL & MOTTO

"Agriculture, Commerce"

Texas

NICKNAME: Lone Star State

Part of Mexico, 1821–1836; independent republic, 1836–1845.

BOUNDARIES

North by Oklahoma; east by Arkansas, Louisiana, and the Gulf of Mexico; south by Mexico; west by New Mexico.

LARGEST CITIES

Houston (1), Dallas (2), San Antonio (3), Fort Worth (4), El Paso (5), Austin (6), Corpus Christi (7).

POPULATION: 11,196,730
RANK: 4th

TIME ZONE

Two westernmost counties: Mountain
Remainder of state: Central

SONG: "Texas, Our Texas"

BIRD

Mockingbird

FLOWER

Bluebonnet

ORIGIN OF NAME

Indian, meaning "Friends"

DISCOVERED

1519 by the Spanish

SETTLED

1682 by the Spanish at Ysleta

AREA & LOCATION

267,339 square miles
2nd in size

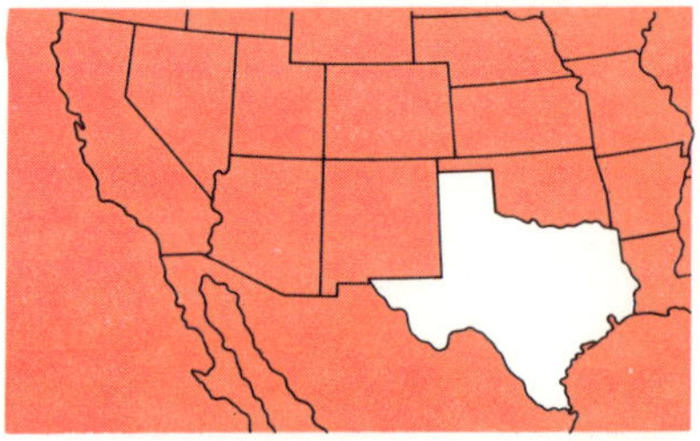

ELEVATION

High: 8,751 feet
Low: sea level

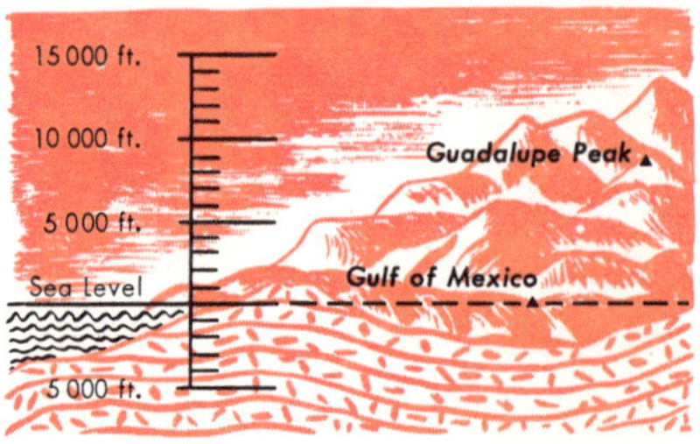

CAPITAL

Austin

ADMITTED TO UNION

1845 as 28th state

SEAL & MOTTO

"Friendship"

Utah

NICKNAME: Beehive State

Part of the Mexican Cession of 1848; included in Provisional State of Deseret from 1848 to 1850; became Territory of Utah, 1850.

BOUNDARIES

North by Idaho, northeast by Wyoming, east by Colorado, south by Arizona, west by Nevada.

LARGEST CITIES

Salt Lake City (1), Ogden (2), Provo (3), Orem (4), Bountiful (5).

POPULATION: 1,059,273
RANK: 36th

TIME ZONE: Mountain

SONG: "Utah, We Love Thee"

BIRD

Sea Gull

FLOWER

Sego Lily

ORIGIN OF NAME

Indian, meaning "High in the Mountains"

DISCOVERED

1540 by the Spanish

SETTLED

1847 by the Mormons at Salt Lake City

AREA & LOCATION

84,916 square miles
11th in size

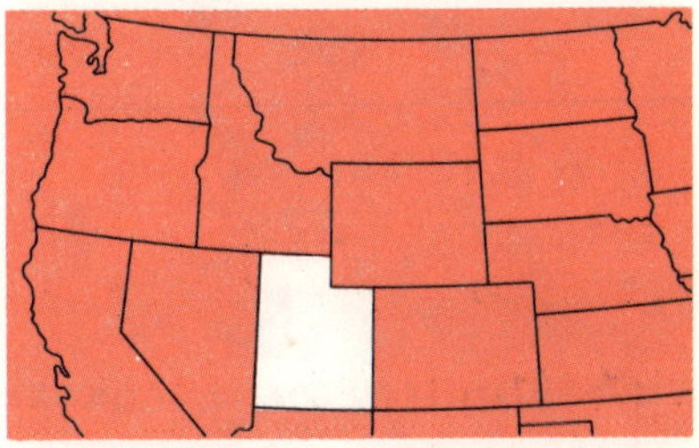

ELEVATION

High: 13,498 feet
Low: 2,000 feet

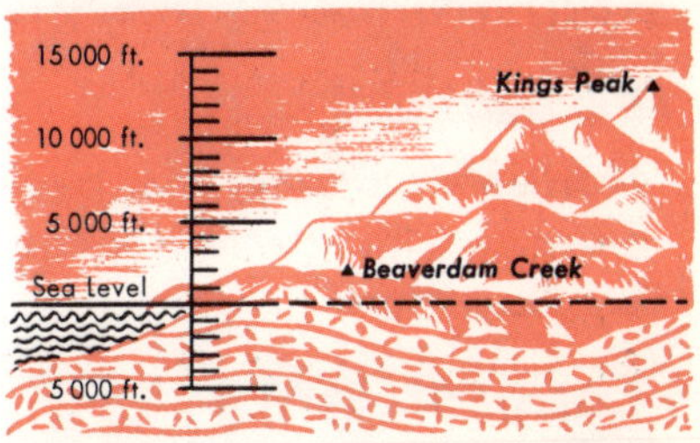

CAPITAL

Salt Lake City

ADMITTED TO UNION

1896 as 45th state

SEAL & MOTTO

"Industry"

Vermont

NICKNAME: Green Mountain State

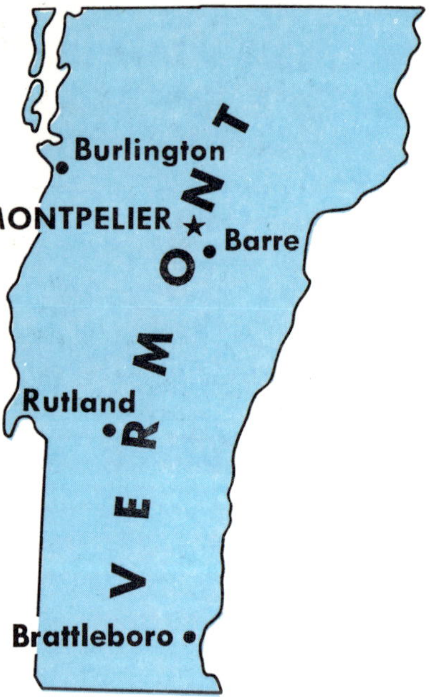

Originally claimed by New Hampshire and New York; independent state from 1777 to 1791.

BOUNDARIES

North by Quebec, east by New Hampshire, south by Massachusetts, west by New York.

LARGEST CITIES

Burlington (1), Rutland (2), Brattleboro (3)

POPULATION: 444,732
RANK: 48th

TIME ZONE: Eastern

SONG: "Hail, Vermont!"

BIRD

Hermit Thrush

FLOWER

Red Clover

ORIGIN OF NAME

French, meaning "Green Mountain"

DISCOVERED

1609 by Champlain (French)

SETTLED

1724 at Fort Dummer by the English

AREA & LOCATION

9,609 square miles
43rd in size

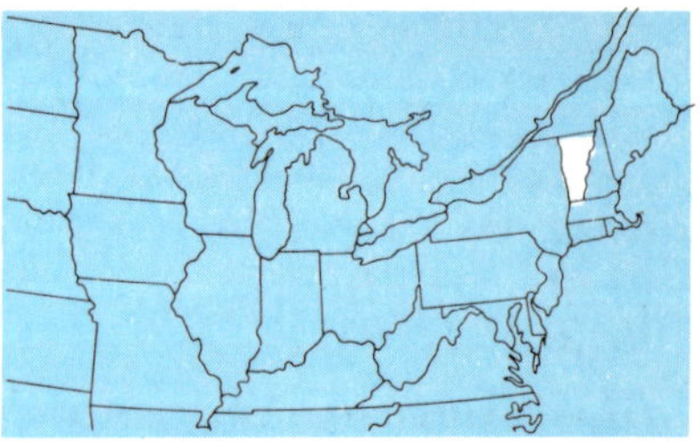

ELEVATION

High: 4,393 feet
Low: 95 feet

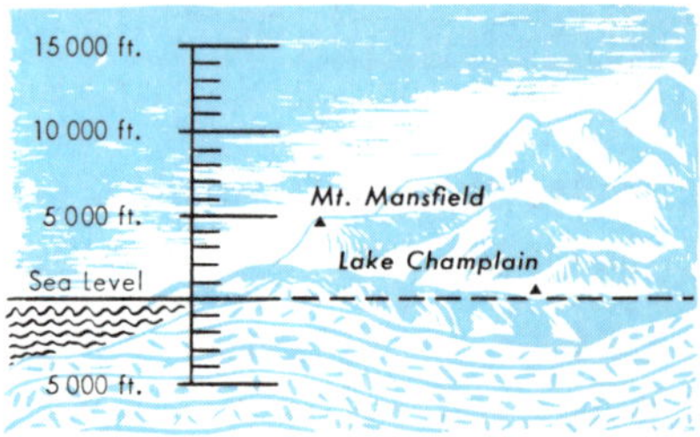

CAPITAL

Montpelier

ADMITTED TO UNION

1791 as 14th state

SEAL & MOTTO

"Freedom and Unity"

Virginia

NICKNAME: Mother of Presidents

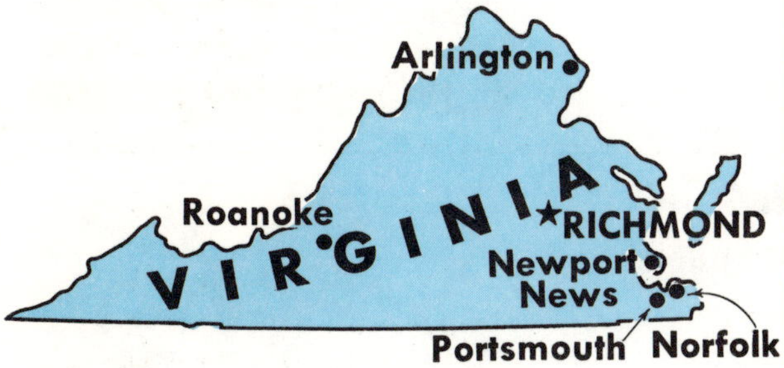

The first popular assembly in America, the house of burgesses, was held in Virginia in 1619. Virginia became a royal colony in 1624; one of the thirteen original states.

BOUNDARIES

Northwest by West Virginia, northeast by Maryland, east by the Atlantic Ocean, south by North Carolina and Tennessee, southwest by Kentucky.

LARGEST CITIES

Norfolk (1), Richmond (2), Virginia Beach (3), Arlington (4), Newport News (5), Hampton (6).

POPULATION: 4,648,494
RANK: 14th

TIME ZONE: Eastern

SONG: "Carry Me Back to Old Virginia"

BIRD

Cardinal

FLOWER

American Dogwood

ORIGIN OF NAME

English, in honor of Elizabeth I, the "Virgin Queen"

DISCOVERED

1520's by Spanish

SETTLED

1607 at Jamestown by English

AREA & LOCATION

40,815 square miles
36th in size

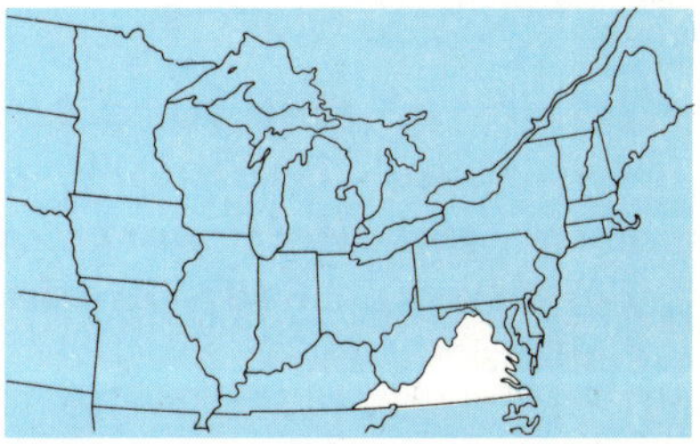

ELEVATION

High: 5,729 feet
Low: sea level

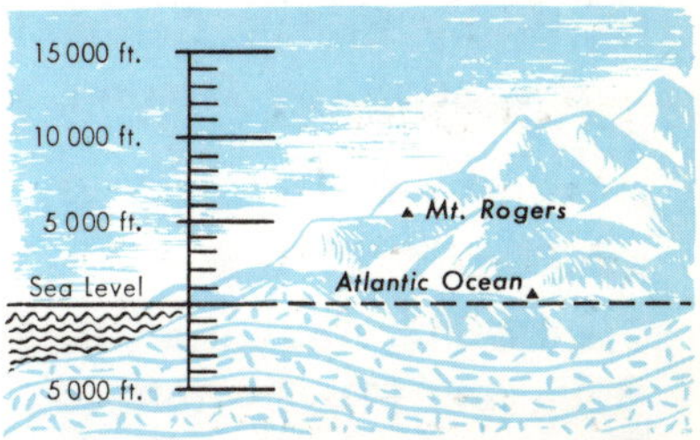

CAPITAL

Richmond

ADMITTED TO UNION

1788 as 10th of the 13 original states

SEAL & MOTTO

"Sic Semper Tyrannis"
("Thus Ever to Tyrants")

Washington

NICKNAME: Evergreen State

Treaty of 1846 fixed the British-American boundary along the 49th parallel; part of Oregon Territory, 1848; made separate territory, 1853.

BOUNDARIES

North by British Columbia, east by Idaho, south by Oregon, west by the Pacific Ocean.

LARGEST CITIES

Seattle (1), Spokane (2), Tacoma (3), Bellevue (4), Everett (5), Lakewood Center (6), Yakima (7), Vancouver (8).

POPULATION: 3,409,169
RANK: 22nd

TIME ZONE: Pacific

SONG: "Washington, My Home"

BIRD

Willow Goldfinch

FLOWER

Western Rhododendron

ORIGIN OF NAME

English, in honor of George Washington

DISCOVERED

1774 by the Spanish

SETTLED

1825 by the English at Vancouver

AREA & LOCATION

68,192 square miles
20th in size

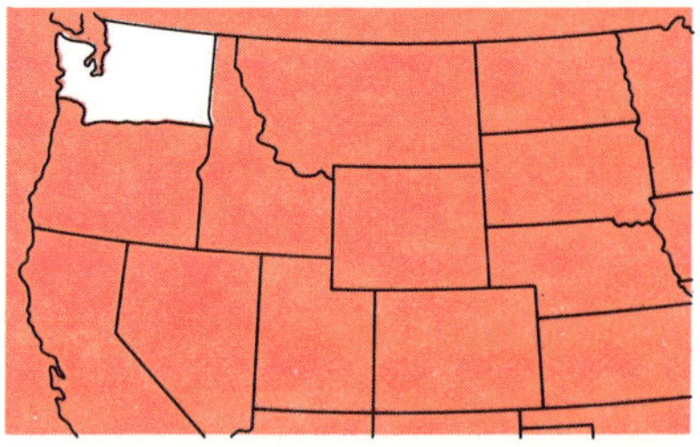

ELEVATION

High: 14,410 feet
Low: sea level

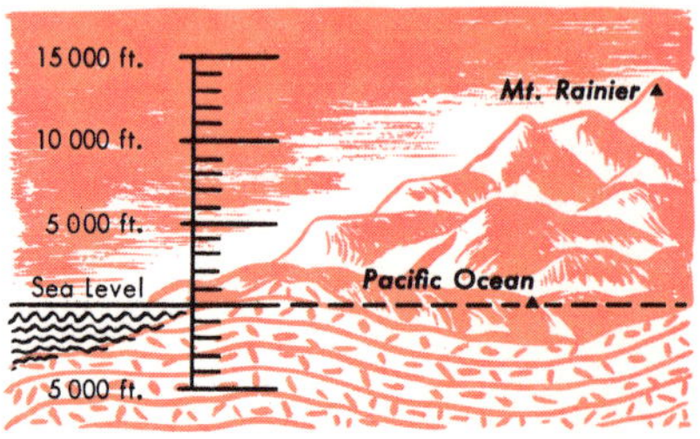

CAPITAL

Olympia

ADMITTED TO UNION

1889 as 42nd state

SEAL & MOTTO

"Al-Ki" ("Bye and Bye")

West Virginia

NICKNAME: Mountain State

Seceded from Virginia in 1861.

BOUNDARIES

North by Pennsylvania and Maryland, east and south by Virginia, southwest by Kentucky, northwest by Ohio.

LARGEST CITIES

Huntington (1), Charleston (2), Wheeling (3), Parkersburg (4), Morgantown (5), Weirton (6), Fairmont (7).

POPULATION: 1,744,237
RANK: 34th

TIME ZONE: Eastern

SONG: "West Virginia Hills"

BIRD

Cardinal

FLOWER

Rhododendron

ORIGIN OF NAME

English, in honor of Elizabeth I, the "Virgin Queen"

DISCOVERED

1671 by the English

SETTLED

1726 by the English at Bunker Hill

AREA & LOCATION

24,181 square miles
41st in size

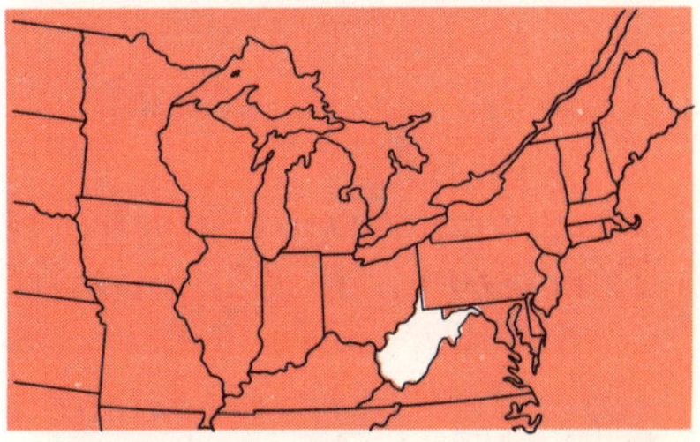

ELEVATION

High: 4,860 feet
Low: 240 feet

CAPITAL

Charleston

ADMITTED TO UNION

1863 as 35th state

SEAL & MOTTO

"Montani Semper Liberi" ("Mountaineers Are Always Free")

Wisconsin

NICKNAME: Badger State

Originally part of the Northwest Territory, 1787, and of Indiana (1800), Illinois (1809), and Michigan (1818) territories; organized as separate territory, 1836.

BOUNDARIES

North by Lake Superior and Michigan, east by Lake Michigan, south by Illinois, west by Iowa and Minnesota.

LARGEST CITIES

Milwaukee (1), Madison (2), Racine (3), Green Bay (4), Kenosha (5).

POPULATION: 4,417,933
RANK: 16th

TIME ZONE: Central

SONG: "On, Wisconsin!"

BIRD

Robin

FLOWER

Wood Violet

ORIGIN OF NAME

Indian, meaning "Gathering of the Waters"

DISCOVERED

1634 by Nicolet (French)

SETTLED

1746 by French at Green Bay

AREA & LOCATION

56,154 square miles
26th in size

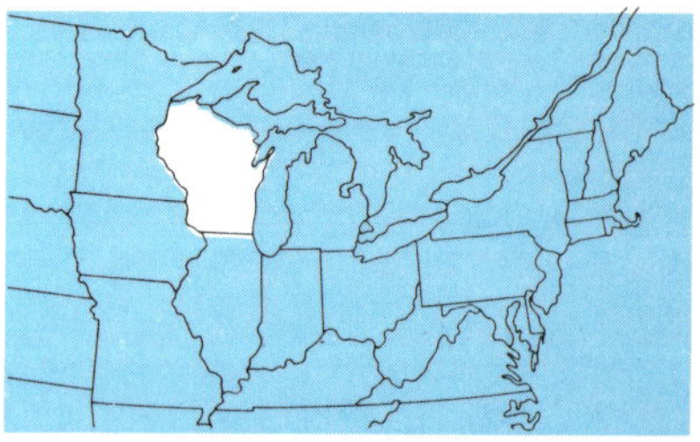

ELEVATION

High: 1,953 feet
Low: 581 feet

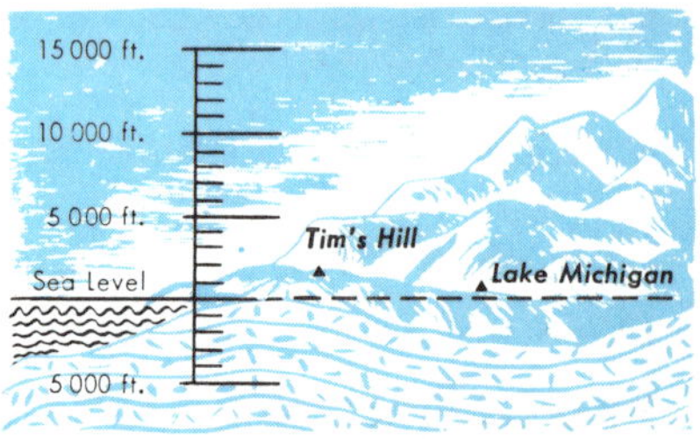

CAPITAL

Madison

ADMITTED TO UNION

1848 as 30th state

SEAL & MOTTO

"Forward"

Wyoming

NICKNAME: Equality State

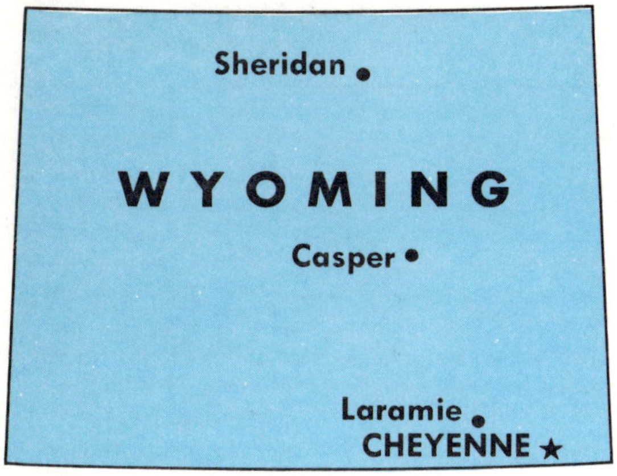

Originally part of Oregon, Idaho, Dakota, and Utah territories; made a separate territory, 1869.

BOUNDARIES

North by Montana, east by South Dakota and Nebraska, south by Colorado and Utah, west by Utah and Idaho.

LARGEST CITIES

Cheyenne (1), Casper (2), Laramie (3).

POPULATION: 332,416
RANK: 49th

TIME ZONE: Mountain

SONG: "Wyoming State Song"

BIRD

Meadowlark

FLOWER

Indian Paint Brush

ORIGIN OF NAME

Indian, meaning "Mountains and Valleys Alternating"

DISCOVERED

1807 by Americans

SETTLED

1834 at Fort Laramie by Americans

AREA & LOCATION

97,914 square miles
9th in size

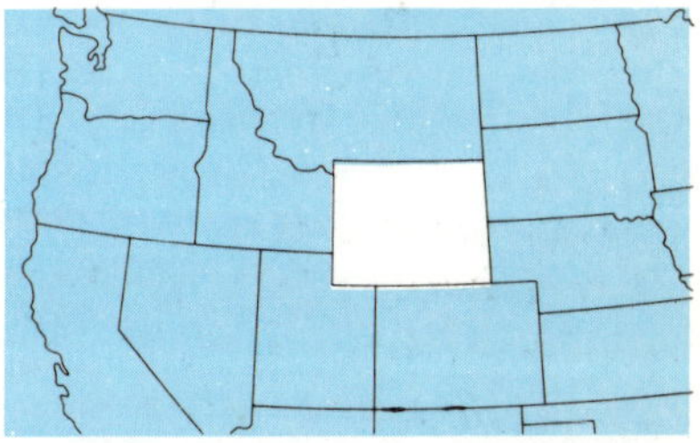

ELEVATION

High: 13,785 feet
Low: 3,100 feet

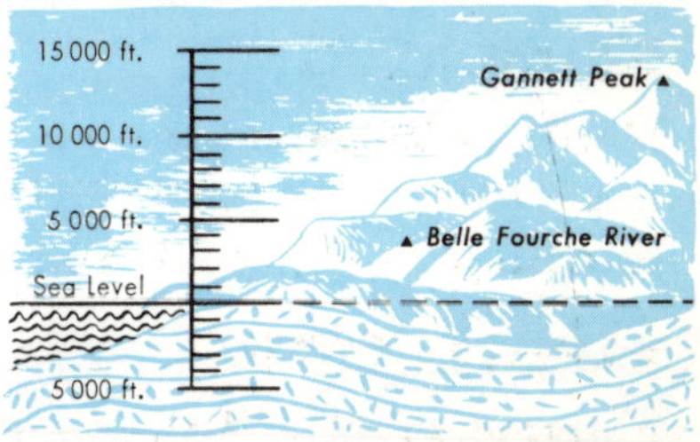

CAPITAL

Cheyenne

ADMITTED TO UNION

1890 as 44th state

SEAL & MOTTO

"Cedant Arma Togae" ("Let Arms Yield to the Gown")

The Declaration of Independence

In Congress, July 4, 1776
The Unanimous Declaration of the Thirteen United States of America

WHEN, in the course of human events, it becomes necessary for one people to dissolve the political bands which have connected them with another, and to assume among the powers of the earth the separate and equal station to which the laws of nature and of nature's God entitle them, a decent respect to the opinions of mankind requires that they should declare the causes which impel them to the separation.

We hold these truths to be self-evident: That all men are created equal; that they are endowed by their Creator with certain unalienable rights; that among these are life, liberty, and the pursuit of happiness; that, to secure these rights, governments are instituted among men, deriving their just powers from the consent of the governed; that whenever any form of government becomes destructive of these ends, it is the right of the people to alter or to abolish it and to institute new government, laying its foundation on such principles, and organizing its powers in such form, as to them shall seem most likely to effect their safety and happiness. Prudence, indeed, will dictate that governments long established should not be changed for light and transient causes; and, accordingly, all experience hath shown that mankind are more disposed to suffer while evils are sufferable, than to right themselves by abolishing the forms to which they are accustomed. But when a long train of abuses and usurpations, pursuing invariably the same object, evinces a design to reduce them under absolute despotism, it is their right, it is their duty, to throw off such government and to provide new guards for their future security. Such has been the patient sufferance of these colonies; and such is now the necessity which constrains them to alter their former systems of government.

The history of the present King of Great Britain is a history of repeated injuries and usurpations, all having in direct object the establishment of an absolute tyranny over these States. To prove this, let facts be submitted to a candid world:

He has refused his assent to laws, the most wholesome and necessary for the public good.

He has forbidden his Governors to pass laws of immediate and pressing importance, unless suspended in their operation till his assent should be obtained; and, when so suspended, he has utterly neglected to attend to them.

He has refused to pass other laws for the accommodation of large districts of people, unless those people would relinquish the right of representation in the Legislature, a right inestimable to them and formidable to tyrants only.

He has called together legislative bodies at places unusual, uncomfortable, and distant from the depository of their public records, for the sole purpose of fatiguing them into compliance with his measures.

He has dissolved representative Houses repeatedly for opposing with manly firmness his invasions on the rights of people.

He has refused for a long time after such dissolutions to cause others to be elected; whereby the legislative powers, incapable of annihilation, have returned to the people at large for their exercise; the State remaining, in the meantime, exposed to all the dangers of invasions from without and convulsions within.

He has endeavored to prevent the population of these States; for that purpose obstructing the laws for naturalization of foreigners, refusing to pass others to encourage their migration hither, and raising the conditions of new appropriations of lands.

He has obstructed the administration of justice by refusing his assent to laws for establishing judiciary powers.

He has made judges dependent on his will alone for the tenure of their offices and the amount and payment of their salaries.

He has erected a multitude of new offices, and sent hither swarms of officers to harass our people and eat out their substance.

He has kept among us, in times of peace, standing armies, without the consent of our Legislatures.

He has affected to render the military independent of, and superior to, the civil power.

He has combined with others to subject us to a jurisdiction foreign to our Constitution and unacknowledged by our laws, giving his assent to their acts of pretended legislation:

For quartering large bodies of armed troops among us;

For protecting them, by a mock trial, from punishment for any murders which they should commit on the inhabitants of these States;

For cutting off our trade with all parts of the world;

For imposing taxes on us without our consent;

For depriving us, in many cases, of the benefits of trial by jury;

For transporting us beyond seas to be tried for pretended offenses;

For abolishing the free system of English laws in a neighboring province, establishing therein an arbitrary government, and enlarging its boundaries so as to render it at once an example and fit instrument for introducing the same absolute rule into these colonies;

For taking away our charters, abolishing our most valuable laws, and altering fundamentally the forms of our governments;

For suspending our own Legislatures, and declaring themselves invested with power to legislate for us in all cases whatsoever.

He has abdicated government here by declaring us out of his protection and waging war against us.

He has plundered our seas, ravaged our coasts, burnt our towns, and destroyed the lives of our people.

He is at this time transporting large armies of foreign mercenaries to complete the works of death, desolation, and tyranny, already begun with circumstances of cruelty and perfidy scarcely paralleled in the most barbarous ages, and totally unworthy the head of a civilized nation.

He has constrained our fellow citizens, taken captive on the high seas, to bear arms against their country, to become the executioners of their friends and brethren, or to fall themselves by their hands.

He has excited domestic insurrections amongst us, and has endeavored to bring on the inhabitants of our frontiers the merciless Indian savages, whose known rule of warfare is an undistinguished destruction of all ages, sexes, and conditions.

In every stage of these oppressions we have petitioned for redress in the most humble terms: our repeated petitions have been answered only by repeated injury. A prince, whose character is thus marked by every act which may define a tyrant, is unfit to be the ruler of a free people.

Nor have we been wanting in attentions to our British brethren. We have warned them from time to time of attempts by their Legislature to extend an unwarrantable jurisdiction over us. We have reminded them of the circumstances of our emigration and settlement here. We have appealed to their native justice and magnanimity, and we have conjured them by the ties of our common kindred to disavow these usurpations which would inevitably interrupt our connections and correspondence. They, too, have been deaf to the voice of justice and of consanguinity. We must, therefore, acquiesce in the necessity which denounces our separation, and hold them, as we hold the rest of mankind, enemies in war; in peace, friends.

We, Therefore, the Representatives of the United States of America, in General Congress assembled, appealing to the Supreme Judge of the world for the rectitude of our intentions, do, in the name and by the authority of the good people of these colonies, solemnly publish and declare that these United Colonies are, and of right ought to be, **Free and Independent States,** that they are absolved from all allegiance to the British Crown, and that all political connection between them and the State of Great Britain is, and ought to be, totally dissolved; and that as free and independent states they have full power to levy war, conclude peace, contract alliances, establish commerce, and to do all other acts and things which independent States may of right do. And for the support of this declaration, with a firm reliance on the protection of Divine Providence, we mutually pledge to each other our lives, our fortunes, and our sacred honor.

JOHN HANCOCK

New Hampshire
JOSIAH BARTLETT
WM. WHIPPLE
MATTHEW THORNTON

Massachusetts Bay
SAML. ADAMS
JOHN ADAMS
ROBT. TREAT PAINE
ELBRIDGE GERRY

Rhode Island
STEP. HOPKINS
WILLIAM ELLERY

Connecticut
RODGER SHERMAN
SAM'EL HUNTINGTON
WM. WILLIAMS
OLIVER WOLCOTT

New York
WM. FLOYD
PHIL. LIVINGSTON
FRANS. LEWIS
LEWIS MORRIS

New Jersey
RICHD. STOCKTON
JNO. WITHERSPOON
FRAS. HOPKINSON
JOHN HART
ABRA. CLARK

Pennsylvania
ROBT. MORRIS
BENJAMIN RUSH
BENJA. FRANKLIN
JOHN MORTON
GEO. CLYMER
JAS. SMITH
GEO. TAYLOR
JAMES WILSON
GEO. ROSS

Delaware
CAESAR RODNEY
GEO. READ
THO. M'KEAN

Maryland
SAMUEL CHASE
WM. PACA
THOS. STONE
CHARLES CARROLL of Carrollton

Virginia
GEORGE WYTHE
RICHARD HENRY LEE
TH. JEFFERSON
BENJA. HARRISON
THOS. NELSON, JR.
FRANCIS LIGHTFOOT LEE
CARTER BRAXTON

North Carolina
WM. HOOPER
JOSEPH HEWES
JOHN PENN

South Carolina
EDWARD RUTLEDGE
THOS. HEYWARD, JUNR
THOMAS LYNCH, JUNR
ARTHUR MIDDLETON

Georgia
BUTTON GWINNETT
LYMAN HALL
GEO. WALTON

United States of America

POPULATION
(1970 census):
203,184,772
RANK: 4th in world

LARGEST CITIES (Metropolitan Areas)
New York (1), Los Angeles (2), Chicago (3), Philadelphia (4), Detroit (5), San Francisco (6), Boston (7), Washington, D.C. (8), Cleveland (9), St. Louis (10).

NATIONAL CAPITAL
Washington, D.C.

NATIONAL SEAL & MOTTO
"E Pluribus Unum"
("One Out of Many")

NATIONAL BIRD
Bald Eagle

The Pledge of Allegiance

I pledge allegiance to the flag of the United States of America,
and to the Republic for which it stands,
one Nation under God, indivisible,
with liberty and justice for all.

The Star-Spangled Banner

O say, can you see by the dawn's early light
What so proudly we hail'd at the twilight's last gleaming,
Whose broad stripes and bright stars, through the perilous fight,
O'er the ramparts we watch'd, were so gallantly streaming?
And the rocket's red glare, the bombs bursting in air,
Gave proof through the night that our flag was still there.
O say, does that star-spangled banner yet wave
O'er the land of the free and the home of the brave?

On the shore dimly seen through the mists of the deep,
Where the foe's haughty host in dread silence reposes,
What is that which the breeze, o'er the towering steep,
As it fitfully blows, half conceals, half discloses?
Now it catches the gleam of the morning's first beam,
In full glory reflected now shines on the stream.
'Tis the star-spangled banner—O long may it wave
O'er the land of the free and the home of the brave.

O thus be it e'er when freemen shall stand
Between their lov'd home and the war's desolation!
Blest with vict'ry and peace may the heav'n rescued land
Praise the Pow'r that hath made and preserved us a nation!
Then conquer we must when our cause it is just,
And this be our motto—"In God is our trust."
And the star-spangled banner in triumph shall wave
O'er the land of the free and the home of the brave.

—*FRANCIS SCOTT KEY*

*The National Education Association in 1912 recommended the above version as the authorized version of "The Star-Spangled Banner." In 1931 Congress enacted a law making the song our national anthem.

The Constitution of the United States

PREAMBLE

WE THE PEOPLE of the United States in order to form a more perfect union, establish justice, insure domestic tranquillity, provide for the common defense, promote the general welfare, and secure the blessings of liberty to ourselves and our posterity, do ordain and establish this Constitution for the United States of America.

THE LEGISLATIVE DEPARTMENT

Article I

Section 1. All legislative powers herein granted shall be vested in a Congress of the United States, which shall consist of a Senate and House of Representatives.

How the House of Representatives Is Formed

Section 2. The House of Representatives shall be composed of members chosen every second year by the people of the several States, and the electors in each State shall have the qualifications requisite for electors of the most numerous branch of the State Legislature.

No person shall be a Representative who shall not have attained to the age of twenty-five years, and been seven years a citizen of the United States, and who shall not, when elected, be an inhabitant of that State in which he shall be chosen.

Representatives and direct taxes shall be apportioned among the several States which may be included within this Union, according to their respective numbers, which shall be determined by adding to the whole number of free persons, including those bound to service for a term of years, and excluding Indians not taxed, three-fifths of all other persons. The actual enumeration shall be made within three years after the first meeting of the Congress of the United States, and within every subsequent term of ten years, in such manner as they shall by law direct. The number of Representatives shall not exceed one for every thirty thousand, but each State shall have at least one Representative; and until such enumeration shall be made, the State of New Hampshire shall be entitled to choose three, Massachusetts eight, Rhode Island and Providence Plantations one, Connecticut five, New York six, New Jersey four, Pennsylvania eight, Delaware one, Maryland six, Virginia ten, North Carolina five, South Carolina five, and Georgia three.

(See also Amendment XIV, Section 2, page 68.)

When vacancies happen in the representation from any State, the executive authority thereof shall issue writs of election to fill such vacancies.

The House of Representatives shall choose their Speaker and other officers; and shall have the sole power of impeachment.

How the Senate Is Formed

Section 3. The Senate of the United States shall be composed of two Senators from each State, chosen by the Legislature thereof, for six years; and each Senator shall have one vote.

Immediately after they shall be assembled in consequence of the first election, they shall be divided as equally as may be into three classes. The seats of the Senators of the first class shall be vacated at the expiration of the second year, of the second class at the expiration of the fourth year, and of the third class at the expiration of the sixth year, so that one-third may be chosen every second year; and if vacancies happen by resignation, or otherwise, during the recess of the Legislature of any State, the Executive thereof may make temporary appointments until the next meeting of the Legislature, which shall then fill such vacancies.

(See also Amendment XVII, page 69.)

No person shall be a Senator who shall not have attained to the age of thirty years, and been nine years a citizen of the United States, and who shall not, when elected, be an inhabitant of that State for which he shall be chosen.

The Vice President of the United States shall be President of the Senate, but shall have no vote unless they be equally divided.

The Senate shall choose their other officers, and also a president *pro tempore*, in the absence of the Vice President, or when he shall exercise the office of President of the United States.

The Senate shall have the sole power to try all

impeachments. When sitting for that purpose, they shall be on oath or affirmation. When the President of the United States is tried, the Chief Justice shall preside, and no person shall be convicted without the concurrence of two-thirds of the members present.

Judgment in cases of impeachment shall not extend further than to removal from office, and disqualification to hold and enjoy any office of honor, trust, or profit under the United States; but the party convicted shall nevertheless be liable and subject to indictment, trial, judgment, and punishment, according to law.

Congressional Elections: Time of Assembling

Section 4. The times, places, and manner of holding elections for Senators and Representatives shall be prescribed in each State by the Legislature thereof; but the Congress may at any time by law make or alter such regulations, except as to the places of choosing Senators.

The Congress shall assemble at least once in every year, and such meeting shall be on the first Monday in December, unless they shall by law appoint a different day.

(See also Amendment XX, Section 2, page 70.)

Rules and Procedure of Congress

Section 5. Each House shall be the judge of the elections, returns, and qualifications of its own members, and a majority of each shall constitute a quorum to do business; but a smaller number may adjourn from day to day, and may be authorized to compel the attendance of absent members, in such manner and under such penalties as each House may provide.

Each House may determine the rules of its proceedings, punish its members for disorderly behavior, and, with the concurrence of two-thirds, expel a member.

Each House shall keep a journal of its proceedings, and from time to time publish the same, excepting such parts as may in their judgment require secrecy; and the yeas and nays of the members of either House on any question shall, at the desire of one-fifth of those present, be entered on the journal.

Neither House, during the session of Congress, shall, without the consent of the other, adjourn for more than three days, nor to any other place than that in which the two Houses shall be sitting.

Privileges and Restrictions of Congressmen

Section 6. The Senators and Representatives shall receive a compensation for their services, to be ascertained by law and paid out of the Treasury of the United States. They shall in all cases, except treason, felony, and breach of the peace, be privileged from arrest during their attendance at the session of their respective Houses, and in going to and returning from the same; and for any speech or debate in either House they shall not be questioned in any other place.

No Senator or Representative shall, during the time for which he was elected, be appointed to any civil office under the authority of the United States, which shall have been created, or the emoluments whereof shall have been increased during such time; and no person holding any office under the United States shall be a member of either House during his continuance in office.

How Federal Laws Are Made

Section 7. All bills for raising revenue shall originate in the House of Representatives; but the Senate may propose or concur with amendments as on other bills.

Every bill which shall have passed the House of Representatives and the Senate shall, before it become a law, be presented to the President of the United States; if he approve he shall sign it, but if not he shall return it with his objections to that House in which it shall have originated, who shall enter the objections at large on their journal and proceed to reconsider it. If after such reconsideration two-thirds of that House shall agree to pass the bill, it shall be sent, together with the objections, to the other House, by which it shall likewise be reconsidered, and if approved by two-thirds of that House, it shall become a law. But in all such cases the votes of both Houses shall be determined by yeas and nays, and the names of the persons voting for and against the bill shall be entered on the journal of each House respectively. If any bill shall not be returned by the President within ten days (Sundays excepted) after it shall have been presented to him, the same shall be a law, in like manner as if he had signed it, unless the Congress by their adjournment prevent its return, in which case it shall not be a law.

Every order, resolution, or vote to which the concurrence of the Senate and House of Representatives may be necessary (except on a question of adjournment) shall be presented to the President of the United States; and before the same shall take effect, shall be approved by him, or being disapproved by him shall be repassed by two-thirds of the Senate and House of Representatives, according to the rules and limitations prescribed in the case of a bill.

Powers Granted to Congress

Section 8. The Congress shall have power to lay and collect taxes, duties, imposts and excises, to pay the debts and provide for the common defense and general welfare of the United States; but all duties, imposts and excises shall be uniform throughout the United States;

To borrow money on the credit of the United States;

To regulate commerce with foreign nations, and among the several States, and with the Indian tribes;

To establish an uniform rule of naturalization, and uniform laws on the subject of bankruptcies throughout the United States;

To coin money, regulate the value thereof and of foreign coin, and fix the standard of weights and measures;

To provide for the punishment of counterfeiting the securities and current coin of the United States;

To establish post offices and post roads;

To promote the progress of science and useful arts, by securing for limited times to authors and inventors the exclusive right to their respective writings and discoveries;

To constitute tribunals inferior to the Supreme Court;

To define and punish piracies and felonies committed on the high seas, and offenses against the law of nations;

To declare war, grant letters of marque and reprisal, and make rules concerning captures on land and water;

To raise and support armies, but no appropriation of money to that use shall be for a longer term than two years;

To provide and maintain a navy;

To make rules for the government and regulation of the land and naval forces;

To provide for calling forth the militia to execute the laws of the Union, suppress insurrections and repel invasions;

To provide for organizing, arming, and disciplining the militia, and for governing such part of them as may be employed in the service of the United States, reserving to the States respectively, the appointment of the officers, and the authority of training the militia according to the discipline prescribed by Congress;

To exercise exclusive legislation, in all cases whatsoever, over such district (not exceeding ten miles square) as may, by cession of particular States, and the acceptance of Congress, become the seat of the government of the United States; and to exercise like authority over all places purchased by the consent of the Legislature of the State in which the same shall be, for the erection of forts, magazines, arsenals, dockyards, and other needful buildings;—and

To make all laws which shall be necessary and proper for carrying into execution the foregoing powers, and all other powers vested by this Constitution in the government of the United States, or in any department or officer thereof.

Powers Denied to the Federal Government

Section 9. The migration or importation of such persons as any of the States now existing shall think proper to admit, shall not be prohibited by the Congress prior to the year one thousand eight hundred and eight, but a tax or duty may be imposed on such importation, not exceeding ten dollars for each person.

The privilege of the writ of *habeas corpus* shall not be suspended, unless when in cases of rebellion or invasion the public safety may require it.

No bill of attainder or *ex post facto* law shall be passed.

No capitation or other direct tax shall be laid, unless in proportion to the census or enumeration hereinbefore directed to be taken.

No tax or duty shall be laid on articles exported from any State.

No preference shall be given by any regulation of commerce or revenue to the ports of one State over those of another; nor shall vessels, bound to or from one State, be obliged to enter, clear, or pay duties in another.

No money shall be drawn from the Treasury, but in consequence of appropriations made by law; and a regular statement and account of the receipts and expenditures of all public money shall be published from time to time.

No title of nobility shall be granted by the United States; and no person holding any office of profit or trust under them shall, without the consent of the Congress, accept of any present, emolument, office, or title, of any kind whatever, from any king, prince, or foreign state.

Powers Denied to State Governments

Section 10. No State shall enter into any treaty, alliance, or confederation; grant letters of marque and reprisal; coin money; emit bills of credit; make anything but gold and silver coin a tender in payment of debts; pass any bill of attainder, *ex post facto* law, or law impairing the obligation of contracts, or grant any title of nobility.

No State shall, without the consent of the Congress, lay any imposts or duties on imports or exports, except what may be absolutely necessary for executing its inspection laws; and the net produce of all duties and imposts, laid by any State on imports or exports, shall be for the use of the Treasury of the United States; and all such laws shall be subject to the revision and control of the Congress.

No State shall, without the consent of Congress, lay any duty of tonnage, keep troops, or ships of war in time of peace, enter into any agreement or compact with another State, or with a foreign power, or engage in war, unless actually invaded or in such imminent danger as will not admit of delay.

THE EXECUTIVE DEPARTMENT

Article II

The President and Vice President

Section 1. The executive power shall be vested in a President of the United States of America. He shall hold his office during the term of four years, and together with the Vice President, chosen for the same term, be elected as follows:

The Electoral College

Each State shall appoint, in such manner as the Legislature thereof may direct, a number of Electors equal to the whole number of Senators and Representatives to which the State may be entitled in the Congress; but no Senator or Representative, or person holding an office of trust or profit under the United States, shall be appointed an Elector.

The Electors shall meet in their respective States, and vote by ballot for two persons, of whom one at least shall not be an inhabitant of the same State with themselves. And they shall make a list of all the persons voted for, and of the number of votes for each; which list they shall sign and certify, and transmit sealed to the seat of the government of the United States, directed to the President of the Senate. The President of the Senate shall, in the presence of the Senate and House of Representatives, open all the certificates, and the votes shall then be counted. The person having the greatest number of votes shall be the President, if such number be a majority of the whole number of Electors appointed; and if there be more than one who have such majority, and have an equal number of votes, then the House of Representatives shall immediately choose by ballot one of them for President; and if no person have a majority, then from the five highest on the list the said House shall in like manner choose the President. But in choosing the President, the votes shall be taken by States, the representation from each State having one vote; a quorum for this purpose shall consist of a member or members from two-thirds of the States, and a majority of all the States shall be necessary to a choice. In every case, after the choice of the President, the person having the greatest number of votes of the Electors shall be the Vice President. But if there should remain two or more who have equal votes, the Senate shall choose from them by ballot the Vice President.

(See also Amendments XII and XX, pages 68 and 70.)

The Congress may determine the time of choosing the Electors, and the day on which they shall give their votes; which day shall be the same throughout the United States.

Qualifications, Succession by Vice President, Salary, and Oath of the President

No person except a natural-born citizen, or a citizen of the United States at the time of the adoption of this Constitution, shall be eligible to the office of President; neither shall any person be eligible to that office who shall not have attained to the age of thirty-five years, and been fourteen years a resident within the United States.

In case of the removal of the President from office, or of his death, resignation, or inability to discharge the powers and duties of the said office, the same shall devolve on the Vice President, and the Congress may by law provide for the case of removal, death, resignation, or inability, both of the President and Vice President, declaring what officer shall then act as President, and such officer shall act accordingly, until the disability be removed or a President shall be elected.

The President shall, at stated times, receive for his services a compensation, which shall neither be increased nor diminished during the period for which he shall have been elected, and he shall not receive within that period any other emolument from the United States, or any of them.

Before he enter on the execution of his office, he shall take the following oath or affirmation: "I do solemnly swear (or affirm) that I will faithfully execute the office of President of the United States, and will, to the best of my ability, preserve, protect, and defend the Constitution of the United States."

Military and Pardoning Powers of the President

Section 2. The President shall be commander in chief of the army and navy of the United States, and of the militia of the several States when called into the actual service of the United States; he may require the opinion, in writing, of the principal officer in each of the executive departments, upon any subject relating to the duties of their respective offices, and he shall have power to grant reprieves and pardons for offenses against the United States, except in cases of impeachment.

Treaties and Appointments by President and Senate

He shall have power, by and with the advice and consent of the Senate, to make treaties, provided two-thirds of the Senators present concur; and he shall nominate, and, by and with the advice and consent of the Senate, shall appoint ambassadors, other public ministers and consuls, judges of the Supreme Court, and all other officers of the United States whose appointments are not herein otherwise provided for, and which shall be established by law; but the Congress may by law vest the appointment of such inferior officers, as they think proper, in the President alone, in the courts of law, or in the heads of departments.

The President shall have power to fill up all vacancies that may happen during the recess of the Senate, by granting commissions which shall expire at the end of their next session.

The Executive and Other Duties of the President

Section 3. He shall from time to time give to the Congress information of the state of the Union, and recommend to their consideration such measures as he shall judge necessary and expedient; he may, on extraordinary occasions, convene both Houses, or either of them, and in case of disagreement between them, with respect to the time of adjournment, he may adjourn them to such time as he shall think proper; he shall receive ambassadors and other public ministers; he shall take care that the laws be faithfully executed, and shall commission all the officers of the United States.

Removal of Executive Officers from Office

Section 4. The President, Vice President, and all civil officers of the United States shall be removed from office on impeachment for, and conviction of, treason, bribery, or other high crimes and misdemeanors.

THE JUDICIAL DEPARTMENT

Article III

The Federal Courts; the Tenure and Salary of Judges

Section 1. The judicial power of the United States shall be vested in one Supreme Court, and in such inferior courts as the Congress may from time to time ordain and establish. The judges, both of the Supreme and inferior courts, shall hold their offices during good behavior, and shall, at stated times, receive for their services a compensation, which shall not be diminished during their continuance in office.

Jurisdiction of Federal Courts in General

Section 2. The judicial power shall extend to all cases in law and equity arising under this Constitution, the laws of the United States, and treaties made, or which shall be made, under their authority; to all cases affecting ambassadors, other public ministers and consuls; to all cases of admiralty and maritime jurisdiction; to controversies to which the United States shall be a party; to controversies between two or more States; between a State and citizens of another State; between citizens of different States; between citizens of the same State claiming lands under grants of different States, and between a State, or the citizens thereof, and foreign states, citizens or subjects.

(See also Amendment XI, page 68.)

Jurisdiction of Supreme Court

In all cases affecting ambassadors, other public ministers and consuls, and those in which a State shall be party, the Supreme Court shall have original jurisdiction. In all the other cases before mentioned, the Supreme Court shall have appellate jurisdiction, both as to law and fact, with such exceptions and under such regulations as the Congress shall make.

Trial by Jury

The trial of all crimes, except in cases of impeachment, shall be by jury; and such trial shall be held in the State where the said crimes shall have been committed; but when not committed within any State, the trial shall be at such place or places as the Congress may by law have directed.

Treason: Its Definition and Punishment

Section 3. Treason against the United States shall consist only in levying war against them, or in adhering to their enemies, giving them aid and comfort. No person shall be convicted of treason unless on the testimony of two witnesses to the same overt act, or on confession in open court.

The Congress shall have power to declare the punishment of treason, but no attainder of treason shall work corruption of blood, or forfeiture except during the life of the person attained.

RELATIONSHIP BETWEEN FEDERAL AND STATE GOVERNMENTS

Article IV

Faith and Credit between States

Section 1. Full faith and credit shall be given in each State to the public acts, records, and judicial proceedings of every other State. And the Congress may by general laws prescribe the manner in which such acts, records, and proceedings shall be proved, and the effect thereof.

Interstate Comity regarding Citizens and Other Persons

Section 2. The citizens of each State shall be entitled to all privileges and immunities of citizens in the several States.

A person charged in any State with treason, felony, or other crime, who shall flee from justice and be found in another State, shall, on demand of the executive authority of the State from which he fled, be delivered up, to be removed to the State having jurisdiction of the crime.

No person held to service or labor in one State, under the laws thereof, escaping into another, shall, in consequence of any law or regulation therein, be discharged from such service or labor, but shall be delivered up on claim of the party to whom such service or labor may be due.

Admission of New States to the Union

Section 3. New States may be admitted by the Congress into this Union; but no new State shall be formed or erected within the jurisdiction of any other State; nor any State be formed by the junction of two or more States, or parts of States, without the consent of the Legislatures of the States concerned as well as of the Congress.

Congress Makes Rules Respecting Government Property

The Congress shall have power to dispose of and make all needful rules and regulations respecting the territory or other property belonging to the United States; and nothing in this Constitution shall be so construed as to prejudice any claims of the United States or of any particular State.

Federal Protection to States

Section 4. The United States shall guarantee to every State in this Union a republican form of government, and shall protect each of them against invasion; and on application of the Legislature, or of the Executive (when the Legislature cannot be convened), against domestic violence.

PROVISIONS FOR AMENDMENTS

Article V

The Congress, whenever two-thirds of both Houses shall deem it necessary, shall propose amendments to this Constitution, or, on the application of the Legislatures of two-thirds of the several States, shall call a convention for proposing amendments, which in either case, shall be valid to all intents and purposes, as part of this Constitution, when ratified by the Legislatures of three-fourths of the several States, or by conventions in three-fourths thereof, as the one or the other mode of ratification may be proposed by the Congress; provided that no amendment which may be made prior to the year one thousand eight hundred and eight shall in any manner affect the first and fourth clauses in the ninth section of the first article; and that no State, without its consent, shall be deprived of its equal suffrage in the Senate.

THE CONSTITUTION, THE SUPREME LAW OF THE LAND

Article VI

Prior Debts

All debts contracted and engagements entered into, before the adoption of this Constitution, shall be as valid against the United States under this Constitution as under the Confederation.

The Supreme Law of the Land and the Obligation of State Judges

This Constitution, and the laws of the United States which shall be made in pursuance thereof; and all treaties made, or which shall be made, under the authority of the United States, shall be the supreme law of the land; and the judges in every State shall be bound thereby, anything in the Constitution or laws of any State to the contrary notwithstanding.

Federal and State Officers Bound by Oath to Support the Constitution

The Senators and Representatives before mentioned, and the members of the several State Legislatures, and all executive and judicial officers, both of the United States and of the several States, shall be bound by oath or affirmation to support this Constitution; but no religious test shall ever be required as a qualification to any office or public trust under the United States.

PROVISIONS FOR RATIFICATION BY STATES

Article VII

The ratification of the conventions of nine states shall be sufficient for the establishment of this Constitution between the States so ratifying the same.

Done in convention by the unanimous consent of the States present, the seventeenth day of September in the year of our Lord one thousand seven hundred and eighty seven, and of the independence of the United States of America the twelfth. In witness whereof we have hereunto subscribed our names.

Attest: WILLIAM JACKSON,
Secretary

GO: WASHINGTON
—Presidt. and Deputy from Virgina

Delaware
GEO: READ
GUNNING BEDFORD, JUN
JOHN DICKINSON
RICHARD BASSETT
JACO: BROOM

Maryland
JAMES McHENRY
DAN OF ST. THOS. JENIFER
DANL. CARROLL

Virginia
JOHN BLAIR
JAMES MADISON, JR.

North Carolina
WM. BLOUNT
RICHD. DOBBS SPAIGHT
HU WILLIAMSON

South Carolina
J. RUTLEDGE
CHARLES COTESWORTH PINCKNEY
CHARLES PINCKNEY
PIERCE BUTLER

Georgia
WILLIAM FEW
ABR BALDWIN

New Hampshire
JOHN LANGDON
NICHOLAS GILMAN

Massachusetts
NATHANIEL GORHAM
RUFUS KING

Connecticut
WM. SAML. JOHNSON
ROGER SHERMAN

New York
ALEXANDER HAMILTON

New Jersey
WIL: LIVINGSTON
DAVID BREARLEY
WM. PATERSON
JONA: DAYTON

Pennsylvania
B. FRANKLIN
THOMAS MIFFLIN
ROBT. MORRIS
GEO. CLYMER
THOS. FITZSIMMONS
JARED INGERSOLL
JAMES WILSON
GOUV MORRIS

THE AMENDMENTS TO THE CONSTITUTION

The first ten amendments to the Constitution, known as "A Bill of Rights," were adopted by the first Congress, called to meet in New York City, March 4, 1789. They were later ratified by the various States, and on December 15, 1791, were made a part of the Constitution.

"The Bill of Rights"

Amendment I

Freedom of Religion, Speech, and the Press; Right of Assembly and Petition

CONGRESS shall make no law respecting an establishment of religion, or prohibiting the free exercise thereof; or abridging the freedom of speech, or of the press, or the right of the people peaceably to assemble, and to petition the government for a redress of grievances.

Amendment II

Right to Keep and Bear Arms

A well regulated militia, being necessary to the security of a free state, the right of the people to keep and bear arms shall not be infringed.

Amendment III

Quartering of Soldiers

No soldier shall in time of peace be quartered in any house without the consent of the owner, nor in time of war, but in a manner to be prescribed by law.

Amendment IV

Regulation of Right of Search and Seizure

The right of the people to be secure in their persons, houses, papers, and effects, against unreasonable searches and seizures, shall not be violated, and no warrants shall issue but upon probable cause, supported by oath or affirmation, and particularly describing the place to be searched and the persons or things to be seized.

Amendment V

Protection for Persons and Their Property

No person shall be held to answer for a capital or otherwise infamous crime, unless on a presentment or indictment of a grand jury, except in cases arising in the land or naval forces, or in the militia, when in actual service in time of war or public danger; nor shall any person be subject for the same offense to be twice put in jeopardy of life or limb; nor shall be compelled in any criminal case to be a witness against himself, nor be deprived of life, liberty, or property, without due process of law; nor shall private property be taken for public use, without just compensation.

Amendment VI

Rights of Persons Accused of Crime

In all criminal prosecutions, the accused shall enjoy the right to a speedy and public trial by an impartial jury of the State and district wherein the crime shall have been committed, which district shall have been previously ascertained by law, and to be informed of the nature and cause of the accusation; to be confronted with the witnesses against him; to have compulsory process for obtaining witnesses in his favor, and to have the assistance of counsel for his defense.

Amendment VII

Right of Trial by Jury in Suits at Common Law

In suits at common law, where the value in controversy shall exceed twenty dollars, the right of trial by jury shall be preserved, and no fact tried by a jury shall be otherwise re-examined in any court of the United States, than according to the rules of the common law.

Amendment VIII

Protection Against Excessive Bail and Punishments

Excessive bail shall not be required, nor excessive fines imposed, nor cruel and unusual punishments inflicted.

Amendment IX

Constitution Does Not List All Individual Rights

The enumeration in the Constitution of certain rights shall not be construed to deny or disparage others retained by the people.

Amendment X

Powers Reserved to the States and the People

The powers not delegated to the United States by the Constitution, nor prohibited by it to the States, are reserved to the States respectively, or to the people.

Amendment XI

Limitation of Power of Federal Courts

The eleventh amendment, adopted by the third Congress, held in Philadelphia, 1794, was made a part of the Constitution, January 8, 1798.

The judicial power of the United States shall not be construed to extend to any suit in law or equity, commenced or prosecuted against one of the United States by citizens of another State, or by citizens or subjects of any foreign state.

(See Article III, Section 2, page 64.)

Amendment XII

Regulation of Electoral College

The twelfth amendment, adopted by the eighth Congress, held in Washington, D. C., 1803, was made a part of the Constitution, September 25, 1804. This amendment was proposed to replace paragraph 3, Section 1, Article II, of the original Constitution.

The Electors shall meet in their respective States and vote by ballot for President and Vice President, one of whom, at least, shall not be an inhabitant of the same State with themselves; they shall name in their ballots the person voted for as President, and in distinct ballots the person voted for as Vice President, and they shall make distinct lists of all persons voted for as President, and of all persons voted for as Vice President, and of the number of votes for each, which lists they shall sign and certify, and transmit sealed to the seat of the government of the United States, directed to the President of the Senate. The President of the Senate shall, in the presence of the Senate and House of Representatives, open all the certificates, and the votes shall then be counted. The person having the greatest number of votes for President shall be the President, if such number be a majority of the whole number of Electors appointed; and if no person have such majority, then from the persons having the highest numbers not exceeding three on the list of those voted for as President, the House of Representatives shall choose immediately, by ballot, the President. But in choosing the President the votes shall be taken by States, the representation from each State having one vote; a quorum or this purpose shall consist of a member or members from two-thirds of the States, and a majority of all the States shall be necessary to a choice. And if the House of Representatives shall not choose a President, whenever the right of choice shall devolve upon them, before the fourth of March next following, then the Vice President shall act as President, as in the case of the death or other constitutional disability of the President. The person having the greatest number of votes as Vice President shall be the Vice President, if such number be a majority of the whole number of Electors appointed; and if no person have a majority, then from the two highest numbers on the list the Senate shall choose the Vice President; a quorum for the purpose shall consist of two-thirds of the whole number of Senators, and a majority of the whole number shall be necessary to a choice. But no person constitutionally ineligible to the office of President shall be eligible to that of Vice President of the United States.

Amendment XIII

Abolition of Slavery

The thirteenth amendment, adopted by the thirty-eighth Congress, held in 1865, was made a part of the Constitution, December 18, 1865.

Section 1. Neither slavery nor involuntary servitude, except as a punishment for crime whereof the party shall have been duly convicted, shall exist within the United States, or any place subject to their jurisdiction.

Section 2. Congress shall have power to enforce this article by appropriate legislation.

Amendment XIV

Guarantee of Protection to All Citizens

The fourteenth amendment, adopted by the thirty-ninth Congress, held in 1866, was made a part of the Constitution, July 28, 1868.

Section 1. All persons born or naturalized in the United States, and subject to the jurisdiction thereof, are citizens of the United States and of the State wherein they reside. No State shall make or enforce any law which shall abridge the privileges or immunities of citizens of the United States; nor shall any State deprive any person of life, liberty, or property, without due process of law; nor deny to any person within its jurisdiction the equal protection of the laws.

Apportionment of Representatives

Section 2. Representatives shall be apportioned among the several States according to their respective numbers, counting the whole number of persons in each State, excluding Indians not taxed. But when the right to vote at any election for the choice of Electors for President and Vice President of the United States, Representatives in Congress, the executive and judicial officers of a State, or the members of the Legislature thereof, is denied to any of the male inhabitants of such State, being twenty-one years of age, and citizens of the United States, or in any way abridged, except for participation in rebellion, or other crime, the basis of representation therein shall be reduced in the proportion which the number of such male citizens shall bear to the whole number of male citizens twenty-one years of age in such State.

(See Article I, Section 2, paragraph 3, page 60.)

Denial of Rights to Hold Public Office

Section 3. No person shall be a Senator or Representative in Congress, or Elector of President and Vice President, or hold any office, civil or military, under the United States, or under any State, who, having previously taken an oath, as a member of Congress, or as an officer of the United States, or as a member of any State Legislature, or as an executive or judicial officer of any State, to support the Constitution of the United States, shall have engaged in insurrection or rebellion against the same, or given aid or comfort to the enemies thereof. But Congress may, by a vote of two-thirds of each House, remove such disability.

Public Debts

Section 4. The validity of the public debt of the United States, authorized by law, including debts incurred for payment of pensions and bounties for services in suppressing insurrection or rebellion, shall not be questioned. But neither the United States nor any State shall assume or pay any debt or obligation incurred in aid of insurrection or rebellion against the United States, or any claim for the loss or emancipation of any slave; but all such debts, obligations, and claims shall be held illegal and void.
Section 5. The Congress shall have power to enforce, by appropriate legislation, the provisions of this article.

Amendment XV

Suffrage Not Denied Because of Race, Color, or Servitude

The fifteenth amendment, adopted by the fortieth Congress, held in 1869, was made a part of the Constitution, March 30, 1870.

Section 1. The right of citizens of the United States to vote shall not be denied or abridged by the United States or by any State on account of race, color, or previous condition of servitude.
Section 2. The Congress shall have power to enforce this article by appropriate legislation.

Amendment XVI

Power to Levy Income Taxes

The sixteenth amendment, adopted by the sixty-first Congress, held in 1909, was made a part of the Constitution, February 25, 1913.

The Congress shall have power to lay and collect taxes on incomes, from whatever source derived, without apportionment among the several States, and without regard to any census or enumeration.

Amendment XVII

Election of Senators by Direct Vote

The seventeenth amendment, adopted by the sixty-second Congress, held in 1912, was made a part of the Constitution, May 31, 1913. This amendment was proposed to replace paragraphs 1 and 2, Section 3, Article I.

The Senate of the United States shall be composed of two Senators from each State, elected by the people thereof, for six years; and each Senator shall have one vote. The electors in each State shall have the qualifications requisite for electors of the most numerous branch of the State Legislatures.

When vacancies happen in the representation of any State in the Senate, the executive authority of such State shall issue writs of election to fill such vacancies: *Provided*, That the Legislature of any State may empower the Executive thereof to make temporary appointments until the people fill the vacancies by election as the Legislature may direct.

This amendment shall not be so construed as to affect the election or term of any Senator chosen before it becomes valid as part of the Constitution.

Amendment XVIII

Prohibition of Manufacture and Sale of Liquor

The eighteenth amendment, adopted by the sixty-fifth Congress, held in 1917, was ratified by three-fourths of the States, and made a part of the Constitution, January 29, 1919.

Section 1. After one year from the ratification of this article the manufacture, sale, or transportation of intoxicating liquors within, the importation thereof into, or the exportation thereof from the United States and all territory subject to the jurisdiction thereof for beverage purposes is hereby prohibited.
Section 2. The Congress and the several States shall have concurrent power to enforce this article by appropriate legislation.
Section 3. This article shall be inoperative unless it shall have been ratified as an amendment to the Constitution by the Legislatures of the several States, as provided in the Constitution, within seven years

from the date of the submission hereof to the States by the Congress.

Amendment XIX

Suffrage Rights Granted to Women

The nineteenth amendment, adopted by the sixty-sixth Congress held in 1919, was made a part of the Constitution, August 26, 1920.

The right of the citizens of the United States to vote shall not be denied or abridged by the United States or by any State on account of sex.

Congress shall have power to enforce this article by appropriate legislation.

Amendment XX

Terms of Office of President, Vice President; Time Congress Shall Assemble

The twentieth amendment, adopted by the seventy-second Congress, held in 1932, was made a part of the Constitution, February 6, 1933.

Section 1. The terms of the President and Vice President shall end at noon on the 20th day of January, and the terms of Senators and Representatives at noon on the 3d day of January, of the years in which such terms would have ended if this article had not been ratified; and the terms of their successors shall then begin.

Section 2. The Congress shall assemble at least once in every year, and such meeting shall begin at noon on the 3d day of January, unless they shall by law appoint a different day.

Section 3. If, at the time fixed for the beginning of the term of the President, the President elect shall have died, the Vice President elect shall become President. If a President shall not have been chosen before the time fixed for the beginning of his term, or if the President elect shall have failed to qualify, then the Vice President elect shall act as President until a President shall have qualified; and the Congress may by law provide for the case wherein neither a President elect nor a Vice President elect shall have qualified, declaring who shall then act as President, or the manner in which one who is to act shall be selected, and such person shall act accordingly until a President or Vice President shall have qualified.

Section 4. The Congress may by law provide for the case of the death of any of the persons from whom the House of Representatives may choose a President, whenever the right of choice shall have devolved upon them, and for the case of the death of any of the persons from whom the Senate may choose a Vice President whenever the right of choice shall have devolved upon them.

Section 5. Sections 1 and 2 shall take effect on the 15th day of October following the ratification of this article.

Section 6. This article shall be inoperative unless it shall have been ratified as an amendment to the Constitution by the Legislatures of three-fourths of the several States within seven years from the date of its submission.

Amendment XXI

Repeal of Prohibition

The twenty-first amendment, adopted by the seventy-second Congress, held in 1933, was made a part of the Constitution, December 5, 1933. *(See page 69.)*

Section 1. The eighteenth article of amendment to the Constitution of the United States is hereby repealed.

Section 2. The transportation or importation into any State, Territory, or possession of the United States for delivery or use therein of intoxicating liquors, in violation of the laws thereof, is hereby prohibited.

Section 3. This article shall be inoperative unless it shall have been ratified as an amendment to the Constitution by conventions in the several States, as provided in the Constitution, within seven years from the date of the submission hereof to the States by the Congress.

Amendment XXII

Limitation of Terms of President and Vice President

The twenty-second amendment, adopted by the seventy-ninth Congress, held in 1947, was made a part of the Constitution, February 26, 1951.

Section 1. No person shall be elected to the office of the President more than twice, and no person who has held the office of President, or acted as President, for more than two years of a term to which some other person was elected President shall be elected to the office of the President more than once. But this article shall not apply to any person holding the office of President when this article was proposed by the Congress, and shall not prevent any person who may be holding the office of President, or acting as President, during the term within which this article becomes operative from holding the office of President or acting as President during the remainder of such term.

Section 2. This article shall be inoperative unless it shall have been ratified as an amendment to the Constitution by the legislatures of three fourths of the several states within seven years from the date of its submission to the states by the Congress.

Amendment XXIII

Right to Vote for President Extended to District of Columbia

The twenty-third amendment, adopted by the eighty-sixth Congress, held in 1960, was made a part of the Constitution, March 29, 1961.

Section 1. The District constituting the seat of Government of the United States shall appoint in such manner as the Congress may direct: A number of electors of President and Vice President equal to the whole number of Senators and Representatives in Congress to which the District would be entitled if it were a State, but in no event more than the least populous State; they shall be in addition to those appointed by the States, but they shall be considered, for the purposes of the election of President and Vice President, to be electors appointed by a State; and they shall meet in the District and perform such duties as provided by the twelfth article of amendment.

Section 2. The Congress shall have the power to enforce this article by appropriate legislation.

Amendment XXIV

Use of Poll Tax in Federal Elections Prohibited

The twenty-fourth amendment, adopted by the eighty-seventh Congress, held in 1962, was made a part of the Constitution, February 4, 1964.

Section 1. The right of citizens of the United States to vote in any primary or other election for President or Vice President, for electors for President or Vice President, or for Senator or Representative in Congress, shall not be denied or abridged by the United States or any State by reason of failure to pay any poll tax or other tax.

Section 2. The Congress shall have power to enforce this article by appropriate legislation.

Amendment XXV

Inability of President to Serve

The twenty-fifth amendment, adopted by the eighty-ninth Congress, held in 1965, was made a part of the Constitution, February 10, 1967.

Section 1. In case of the removal of the President from office or of his death or resignation, the Vice President shall become President.

Section 2. Whenever there is a vacancy in the office of the Vice President, the President shall nominate a Vice President who shall take office upon confirmation by a majority vote of both Houses of Congress.

Section 3. Whenever the President transmits to the President pro tempore of the Senate and the Speaker of the House of Representatives his written declaration that he is unable to discharge the powers and duties of his office, and until he transmits to them a written declaration to the contrary, such powers and duties shall be discharged by the Vice President as Acting President.

Section 4. Whenever the Vice President and a majority of either the principal officers of the executive departments or of such other body as Congress may by law provide, transmit to the President pro tempore of the Senate and the Speaker of the House of Representatives their written declaration that the President is unable to discharge the powers and duties of his office, the Vice President shall immediately assume the powers and duties of the office as Acting President.

Thereafter, when the President transmits to the President pro tempore of the Senate and the Speaker of the House of Representatives his written declaration that no inability exists, he shall resume the powers and duties of his office unless the Vice President and a majority of either the principal officers of the executive department or of such other body as Congress may by law provide, transmit within four days to the President pro tempore of the Senate and the Speaker of the House of Representatives their written declaration that the President is unable to discharge the powers and duties of his office. Thereupon Congress shall decide the issue, assembling within forty-eight hours for that purpose if not in session. If the Congress, within twenty-one days after receipt of the latter written declaration, or, if Congress is not in session, within twenty-one days after Congress is required to assemble, determines by two-thirds vote of both Houses that the President is unable to discharge the powers and duties of his office, the Vice President shall continue to discharge the same as Acting President; otherwise, the President shall resume the powers and duties of his office.

Amendment XXVI

Suffrage Rights Granted to Eighteen-Year Olds

The twenty-sixth amendment, adopted by the ninety-first Congress, held in 1971, was made a part of the Constitution, June 30, 1971.

Section 1. The right of citizens of the United States, who are eighteen years of age or older, to vote shall not be denied or abridged by the United States or by any State on account of age.

Section 2. The Congress shall have power to enforce this article by appropriate legislation.

PACIFIC STANDARD TIME
MOUNTAIN STANDARD TIME
CENT
C A
P A C I F I C O C E A N
130°
125°
120°
115°
110°
105°
100°
45°
40°
35°
30°
Vancouver
Calgary
Regina
Seattle
Olympia
Tacoma
Spokane
WASHINGTON
Portland
Columbia
Salem
Eugene
OREGON
CASCADE RANGE
ROCKY MOUNTAINS
COAST RANGES
IDAHO
Boise
Snake
River
Idaho Falls
Great Falls
Helena
Butte
MONTANA
Missouri
River
Yellowstone River
Billings
NORTH DAKO
Bismarck
SOUTH DAKO
Pierre
Miss
WYOMING
Casper
Cheyenne
North
Platte
NEBRAS
Great Salt Lake
Ogden
Salt Lake City
Provo
WASATCH RANGE
UTAH
NEVADA
Carson City
Sacramento
San Francisco
San Francisco Bay
Berkeley
Oakland
SIERRA NEVADA
CALIFORNIA
Mt. Whitney
Las Vegas
Hoover Dam
River
GRAND CANYON
Greeley
South
Denver
COLORADO
Pueblo
KAN
Ark
Los Angeles
Long Beach
San Diego
Colorado
ARIZONA
Phoenix
Tucson
Santa Fe
Albuquerque
NEW MEXICO
Oklahoma
Amarillo
OK
Lubbock
Fort Wo
El Paso
Rio
Grande
TEX
Austi
San Antonio
MEX.
Browns
25°
ASIA
SOVIET UNION
160°
180°
ARCTIC OCEAN
Point Barrow
70°
60°
BERING STRAIT
ARCTIC CIRCLE
Nome
Yukon
River
Mt. McKinley 20,320 Ft.
Fairbanks
BERING SEA
Anchorage
Palmer
Seward
CANADA
GULF OF ALASKA
Juneau
Sitka
Kodiak
Ketchikan
ALEUTIAN ISLANDS
ALASKA
0 100 200 300 Miles
140°
KAUAI
OAHU
Honolulu
MAUI
20°
Mauna Kea
Hilo
HAWAII
0 25 50 100 150 200 Miles
MIDWAY I.
170°
PACIFIC OCEAN
HAWAIIAN ISLANDS
TROPIC OF CANCER
HAWAII

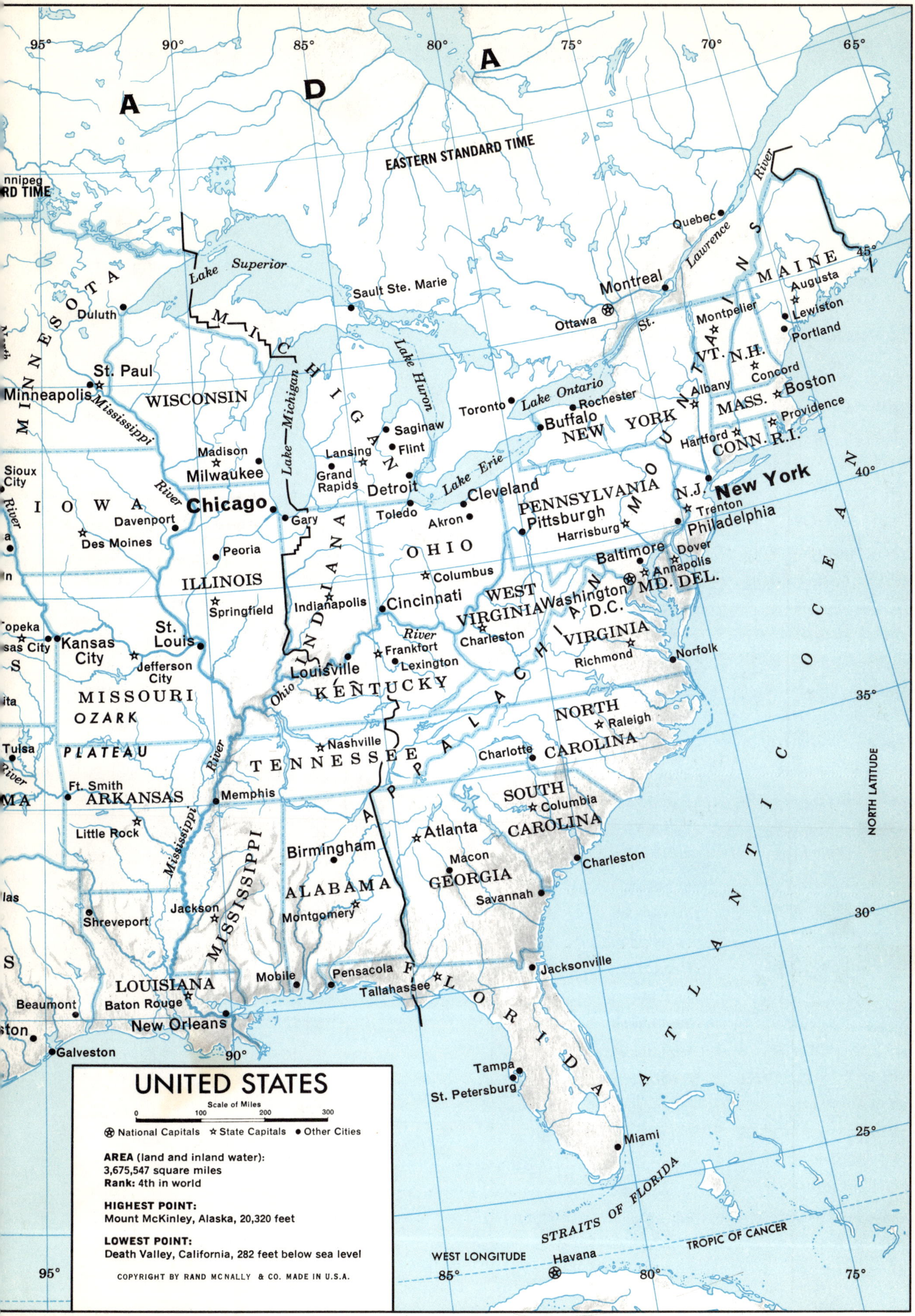
UNITED STATES
Scale of Miles
0 100 200 300
National Capitals
State Capitals
Other Cities
AREA (land and inland water):
3,675,547 square miles
Rank: 4th in world
HIGHEST POINT:
Mount McKinley, Alaska, 20,320 feet
LOWEST POINT:
Death Valley, California, 282 feet below sea level
COPYRIGHT BY RAND McNALLY & CO. MADE IN U.S.A.
95°
90°
85°
80°
75°
70°
65°
45°
40°
35°
30°
25°
WEST LONGITUDE
NORTH LATITUDE
TROPIC OF CANCER
A
D
A
EASTERN STANDARD TIME
nnipeg
RD TIME
Lake Superior
Lake Michigan
Lake Huron
Lake Erie
Lake Ontario
St. Lawrence River
Mississippi River
Ohio River
ATLANTIC OCEAN
STRAITS OF FLORIDA
APPALACHIAN MOUNTAINS
OZARK PLATEAU
MINNESOTA
WISCONSIN
MICHIGAN
IOWA
ILLINOIS
INDIANA
OHIO
PENNSYLVANIA
NEW YORK
VT.
N.H.
MAINE
MASS.
CONN.
R.I.
N.J.
MD.
DEL.
WEST VIRGINIA
VIRGINIA
KENTUCKY
MISSOURI
TENNESSEE
NORTH CAROLINA
SOUTH CAROLINA
ARKANSAS
MISSISSIPPI
ALABAMA
GEORGIA
LOUISIANA
FLORIDA
Duluth
St. Paul
Minneapolis
Madison
Milwaukee
Chicago
Gary
Sault Ste. Marie
Lansing
Grand Rapids
Saginaw
Flint
Detroit
Toledo
Cleveland
Akron
Columbus
Cincinnati
Indianapolis
Peoria
Springfield
Davenport
Des Moines
Sioux City
Kansas City
Jefferson City
St. Louis
Louisville
Frankfort
Lexington
Nashville
Memphis
Ft. Smith
Little Rock
Tulsa
Shreveport
Jackson
Baton Rouge
New Orleans
Beaumont
Galveston
Mobile
Pensacola
Tallahassee
Montgomery
Birmingham
Atlanta
Macon
Savannah
Jacksonville
Tampa
St. Petersburg
Miami
Havana
Charleston
Columbia
Charlotte
Raleigh
Norfolk
Richmond
Washington D.C.
Baltimore
Annapolis
Dover
Philadelphia
Trenton
Harrisburg
Pittsburgh
New York
Hartford
Providence
Boston
Concord
Albany
Montpelier
Portland
Lewiston
Augusta
Buffalo
Rochester
Toronto
Ottawa
Montreal
Quebec

Presidents of the United States

NAME	PARTY	BIRTHPLACE	DATE OF BIRTH	TERM
1. GEORGE WASHINGTON	Federal	Virginia	February 22, 1732	1789–1797
2. JOHN ADAMS	Federal	Massachusetts	October 30, 1735	1797–1801
3. THOMAS JEFFERSON	Democratic-Republican	Virginia	April 13, 1743	1801–1809
4. JAMES MADISON	Democratic-Republican	Virginia	March 16, 1751	1809–1817
5. JAMES MONROE	Democratic-Republican	Virginia	April 28, 1758	1817–1825
6. JOHN QUINCY ADAMS	Democratic-Republican	Massachusetts	July 11, 1767	1825–1829
7. ANDREW JACKSON	Democratic	South Carolina	March 15, 1767	1829–1837
8. MARTIN VAN BUREN	Democratic	New York	December 5, 1782	1837–1841
9. WILLIAM H. HARRISON	Whig	Virginia	February 9, 1773	1841
10. JOHN TYLER	Whig	Virginia	March 29, 1790	1841–1845
11. JAMES K. POLK	Democratic	North Carolina	November 2, 1795	1845–1849
12. ZACHARY TAYLOR	Whig	Virginia	November 24, 1784	1849–1850
13. MILLARD FILLMORE	Whig	New York	January 7, 1800	1850–1853
14. FRANKLIN PIERCE	Democratic	New Hampshire	November 23, 1804	1853–1857
15. JAMES BUCHANAN	Democratic	Pennsylvania	April 23, 1791	1857–1861
16. ABRAHAM LINCOLN	Republican	Kentucky	February 12, 1809	1861–1865
17. ANDREW JOHNSON	Republican	North Carolina	December 29, 1808	1865–1869
18. ULYSSES S. GRANT	Republican	Ohio	April 27, 1822	1869–1877
19. RUTHERFORD B. HAYES	Republican	Ohio	October 4, 1822	1877–1881
20. JAMES A. GARFIELD	Republican	Ohio	November 19, 1831	1881
21. CHESTER A. ARTHUR	Republican	Vermont	October 5, 1830	1881–1885
22. GROVER CLEVELAND	Democratic	New Jersey	March 18, 1837	1885–1889
23. BENJAMIN HARRISON	Republican	Ohio	August 20, 1833	1889–1893
24. GROVER CLEVELAND	Democratic	New Jersey	March 18, 1837	1893–1897
25. WILLIAM McKINLEY	Republican	Ohio	January 29, 1843	1897–1901
26. THEODORE ROOSEVELT	Republican	New York	October 27, 1858	1901–1909
27. WILLIAM H. TAFT	Republican	Ohio	September 15, 1857	1909–1913
28. WOODROW WILSON	Democratic	Virginia	December 28, 1856	1913–1921
29. WARREN G. HARDING	Republican	Ohio	November 2, 1865	1921–1923
30. CALVIN COOLIDGE	Republican	Vermont	July 4, 1872	1923–1929
31. HERBERT C. HOOVER	Republican	Iowa	August 10, 1874	1929–1933
32. FRANKLIN D. ROOSEVELT	Democratic	New York	January 30, 1882	1933–1945
33. HARRY S. TRUMAN	Democratic	Missouri	May 8, 1884	1945–1953
34. DWIGHT D. EISENHOWER	Republican	Texas	October 14, 1890	1953–1961
35. JOHN F. KENNEDY	Democratic	Massachusetts	May 29, 1917	1961–1963
36. LYNDON B. JOHNSON	Democratic	Texas	August 27, 1908	1963–1969
37. RICHARD M. NIXON	Republican	California	January 9, 1913	1969–1974
38. GERALD R. FORD	Republican	Nebraska	July 14, 1913	1974–1977
39. JAMES E. CARTER	Democratic	Georgia	October 1, 1924	1977–